Sexuality

An Empowerment Perspective

स्त्री शक्ति
Shtrii Shakti

Kathmandu

S2. 2012. *Sexuality: An Empowerment Perspective.* Kathmandu: Shtrii Shakti.

Published by
Shtrii Shakti (S2)
PO Box 23111, Kathmandu, Nepal
Phone/Fax: 977-01-4446053 / 4433698
Email: shtriishakti@s2.wlink.com.np
www.shtriishakti.org

ISBN 978-9937-2-3912-7

Graphic design, cover and printing:
PagePerfect, Kathmandu, Nepal; Ph: 4442191

Foreword

Shtrii Shakti (S2) works with a holistic view—out to reach not just the head but also the heart or the spiritual centre, not just thinking but also feeling of a person. In other words this institution is guided by the principle of 3 Es: energy, emotion and esteem. Energy, as in physical energy and vitality, a powerful physical force. Emotional energy, a powerful creative force. Esteem or positive thinking as a life-directing force!

This study represents another step in the direction of our holistic approach to addressing or looking at an issue of importance as it examines the links between sexuality and women's empowerment.

Despite the many advances made with regard to women's empowerment in Nepal, including in the economic, political and reproductive health sectors, our movement has failed until now, to recognize the importance of women's sexuality to the continued empowerment of women, and it is a failure which remains, until resolved, highly delimiting.

Before continuing though, we must attempt to understand what is meant by sexuality. First and foremost, our sexuality is tied up most intimately and essentially with our humanity. Not one of us can be a human being without possessing sexuality; nor can any one of us possess sexuality without being a human being. As such, for every person here, our sexuality remains something that is both unique and individual in one's very own self. Though no universal definition of sexuality exists and no dictionary definition proves sufficient, to provide for a working terminology, let's turn towards the one provided by the World Health Organization (WHO), which defines sexuality as: 'The central aspect of being human, encompassing sex, gender identities/roles, sexual orientation, eroticism, pleasure, intimacy, and reproduction.'

Even in accepting the WHO definition, a variety of perceptions of sexuality exists.

Anthropological Perspective
The first of these is the anthropological perspective, which remains closely aligned with the social constructionist theory. These perspectives regard sexuality as primarily a social construct; everything from our actions to our behaviours, from our roles to our desires, has been a structure of society, including economic and cultural elements, and is directly responsible for producing what has become the accepted norms of sexuality.

Feminist Perspective
Moving in a similar vein to this structural approach is the feminist perspective. This perspective finds women's sexuality as something established within a society already disposed to difference in power based on gender. The men who possess the power within the patriarchy define sexuality for women. They establish what is acceptable and what is not, what is clean and what is dirty, and what is pure and what is tainted.

Biomedical Perspective
Differing from these approaches is the biomedical perspective, and in this perspective sexuality is reduced simply to a combination of hormones and organs. It expands naturally from the right combinations of hormones interacting with the proper cells found in organs in just the proper placement. From this cellular construct spawned the difference in sexuality between men and women.

Mythological Perspective
Older than all these and until only recently somewhat unexamined is the mythological (*tantrically* chronicled) approach. Prior to the studies of sociology and psychology, human beings operated within their societies according to the established myths, legends and tales, which both encouraged and condemned specific behaviours, championing or damning legendary heroes and villains as exemplifiers of either virtue or vice.

While each of these perspectives offers some understanding of a unified theory of sexuality, not one is complete within itself. Sexuality rather is something that should be seen as a combination of biology and society, of myth and power, and women's sexuality in Nepal serves as a perfect example.

As our research has shown, women in Nepal have been so exposed to systemic patriarchy, that it has become ingrained into their very own selves. A woman's being remains consistently and constantly controlled by a society which defines them as subservient and as less than their male counterparts. The consequences of this ever-present patriarchy manifest themselves in the responses gathered in our initial surveys. Women were, for the most part, unaware of their own rights as human beings, especially with regard to sexuality and reproductive health. Patriarchy drives women into silence and hesitancy in open discussion of their own sexuality and discourages further learning, both about their own sexuality and about sexual health generally. This further leads to misunderstanding and misconceptions of sexual biology and, in particular, to the transmission of sexually transmitted diseases, most worrisome of which is HIV/AIDS. In doing this, society is attempting to separate the woman from her sexuality, delegating her to no more than something to be objectified.

What is needed now for continued empowerment of the women of Nepal is an attitudinal shift regarding their own sexuality. But this shift can only be brought about when they are no longer ignorant about, or ashamed of, their sexuality. By bringing them into open discussion, women can begin to recognize the value of their unique sexuality, and elevating their sexuality is almost overpowering. In our myths and legends, we are goddesses and creative forces, the Divine Mother and the source of life. She is **Shakti**— the third divinity of the triad, the archetypal Force representing in her many forms the 'female energy' of the universe (Fritjof Capra). We are uniquely tied to the creation and perpetuation of the universe. Thinking of women's sexuality while being mindful of our historical-cultural and spiritual backgrounds, the patriarchal assertions seem a travesty at best. What creates life it calls unclean; what carried life it calls impure. Patriarchy attempts to drive our sexualities into the darkness, demeaning us as human beings. It places demands upon women to hide their sexuality, while men abound with their libertine licentiousness.

Changing attitudes remains far from easy. It is indeed a challenge. Before we can even begin this task, we must create safe spaces for women to speak out openly, honestly and loudly about their sexuality. Only then can we move on to recognize the patriarchy inherent in women's sexuality and begin to remove its painful stain.

We must work with women to defeat the destructive elements of patriarchy, which have become so internalized into our sexuality. For far too long, women have regarded their sexuality as something to be hidden, as something that is not their own but rather belonging to their husbands and to their families. By allowing for open and honest discussions of this much contested issue, we allow women the opportunity to reclaim their right to **BE**, and in doing so, we are also creating a space for them to return to the fullness of their own selves.

In an attempt to begin this discussion and the resulting shift in attitude regarding sexuality, S2 has initiated this exercise.

Indira Shrestha
Chief Executive
S2

Acknowledgement

'Looking at Sexuality in Relation to Women's Empowerment within the Nepali Context' is a study dedicated to all Nepali women. It was carried out by S2 with technical and financial support of the Ford Foundation, New Delhi. S2 would like to express its appreciation of its partner organization, Chartare Yuva Club, Baglung, project target community studied and all stakeholders, local, district and national, for contributing productively in different phases of the project. This study is dedicated to them. We would also like to thank all our Gender Master Trainers for their inputs in successful completion of this work.

S2 would like to gratefully acknowledge the professional contributions of all resource persons and subject-matter specialists, viz Advocate Sabin Shrestha, Pinky Singh Rana, Sunil Babu Pant, Dr Khem Bahadur Karki and Dr Sudha Basnet. Similarly, special thanks to Dr Indira Basnet, Dr Chattr Amatya and Matina Shrestha.

To Sanjaya Khanal, the technical backstopper of this undertaking, S2 gratefully extends its appreciation for his unconditional dedication and drive to oversee the entirety of this challenging research.

The entire S2 team, especially Shanti Manandhar, focal staff for this study, deserve applause and a great 'thank you' for their hard work and sincerity in carrying out different levels of responsibilities assigned to them.

Thank you all!!

Indira Shrestha
Chief Executive
S2

Contents

Abbreviations and Acronyms

AIDS	Acquired Immunodeficiency Syndrome
ART	Anti-Retroviral Treatment
CEDAW	Convention on the Elimination of all Forms of Discrimination against Women
FCHVs	Female Community Health Volunteers
GO	Government Organization
HIV	Human Immunodeficiency Virus
LGBT	Lesbians, Gays, Bisexuals and Transgender
NGO	Non-Governmental Organization
NDHS	Nepal Demographic and Health Survey
RH	Reproductive Health
SLC	School Leaving Certificate
STD	Sexually Transmitted Disease
S2	Shtrii Shakti
TYIP	Three-Year Interim Plan
VDC	Village Development Committee
WHO	World Health Organization

Executive Summary

Background

Sexuality refers to the whole way a person goes about expressing her/himself as a sexual being, including innate attributes such as sexual desires, roles, identities and orientations. It represents a complex, rich and subtle world of experiences. What constitutes 'sexuality' can change, depending on time and place, and it encompasses sex, gender identities and roles, sexual orientation, pleasure, intimacy and reproduction. It can be experienced and expressed through thoughts, fantasies, desires, beliefs, attitudes, values, behaviours, practices and so forth. It is influenced by the interactions of biological, psychological, social, economic, political, cultural, ethical, legal, historical, religious and spiritual factors.

Norms and behaviours aimed at regulating women's bodies and their sexuality have been features of all major civilizations. Such practices, legitimized by the male elite, subordinated women to the 'dominant' male sexuality by applying 'disciplinary technologies' and surveillance practices onto the bodies of women. Predominantly patriarchal Nepali society is governed by upper class or caste men at the family, community and state levels, and has over time constructed and enforced behavioural norms for women which emphasize the suppressing of sexuality. The central goal of such norms was to instil fidelity in women. A woman violating such norms caused her family, in-laws and kin dishonour, embarrassment and shame. This sexual subjugation and control of women has remained the prime cause of their disempowerment in multiple dimensions of life. Yet, sexuality is generally considered to be a taboo subject and is not to be not discussed openly. So far, women's empowerment discourses in Nepal have been focusing on upgrading women's social and economic status through social, economic and political empowerment. Little thought has been given to the connections between women's empowerment, development and sexuality.

Globally, and also in South Asia, sexuality discourses have already made pathways. There is an ongoing debate stressing the necessity for women to be able to control all aspects of their lives and sexuality, and, against this backdrop (and in the context of the building of 'New Nepal'), various groups and actors across the country also need to look into the empowering and liberating possibilities of this discussion. Accordingly, Shtrii Shakti (S2) carried out this study with that end in mind.

The study was designed with six specific objectives: 1) to break the silence around the issue of sexuality in the community and improve opportunities for open discussion; 2) to look at sexuality from different dimensions, especially from an empowerment perspective; 3) to educate teachers, community leaders, women and men in order to change public opinion and cultivate respect for women's sexuality; 4) to disseminate sexuality-related knowledge, understanding and services in the community; 5) to enhance the capacity of existing gender, reproductive health and informal education trainers in relation to sexuality; and 6) to provide policy recommendations on issues of female sexuality.

This situation analysis is mainly based on a desk review of secondary sources of information and field work carried out in the areas of three village development committees (VDCs) of Baglung district, Lekhani, Bhim Pokhara and Bhiun, which collected some impressions from the grass roots level. As systematic and comprehensive empirical studies in matters of sexuality have not been done in the past, this study has had to rely on the scarce information collected from diverse sources. Again, due to the diverse regional, ethnic, religious and other background characteristics of the population, the available information may not capture their subtle uniqueness and experiences.

Theories, Approaches and Perspectives

Sexuality is a contested topic and is constructed differently in different parts of the world at different times, resulting in different perspectives and approaches. For anthropologists, particular versions of sexual practices, sexual identities and orientations are the impressions of the surrounding society, its way of life, norms and belief systems. The role of culture and learning in shaping sexual behaviour is emphasized and universalism and essentialism are rejected. Although 'sexual drive' is biologically determined, culture can encourage or discourage sexual expressions and acts, attitudes and relationships.

The analysis of power relations is central to the feminist perspectives of sexuality. Drawing on the traditional concept of power as a repressive force, they have sought explanations for women's oppression in patriarchal social structures. There is diversity within feminist scholarship with regard to sexuality and sexual rights. Radical feminists emphasize that ultimately it is men who abuse, harass and rape women and who buy and use pornography and commercial sex. The subordination of women is perpetuated primarily through men's control over the bodies and sexuality of women. Pro-feminist men's studies also highlight the issue of power, but argue that the social construction of gender roles is invisible and men are often unaware of their power and complicity in the process of subordination. Therefore, feminists emphasize sexual autonomy and fulfilment as part of a wider political struggle against patriarchy.

A biomedical approach considers sexuality as a pre-social and biological entity. It tends to reduce women's sexuality to physiological characteristics and organic and reproductive processes. Age, hormone level, specific illnesses and malfunctioning body parts are its concerns and are diagnosed through clinical procedures, after which treatment is prescribed. Sexual orientation, expressions and behaviours are attributed to a genetic predisposition that is biologically determined. The medical profession views a woman's body as a patient, and gives instructions about aspects of personal hygiene, excluding intimate bodily experiences.

For the social construction theory, sexuality is a social construction that is discursively produced as an instrument of social and political control. In modern society, the behaviour of individuals and groups is controlled by establishing standards of normality, which are disseminated through a range of 'scientific administrative discourses' such as criminology, medicine, psychology and psychiatry, which generate and claim 'truth'. Through normalization and classification, people are made self-regulating individuals requiring less and less external enforcement. The seemingly natural masculine gender and heterosexual desire in male bodies is culturally constructed through the repetition of stylized acts over time. Accordingly, the three categories of sex, gender and sexuality are 'performative'. However, the performance is not voluntary but confined to the spaces created by 'regulative discourses', which in advance determine the possibility of performance.

The mythological perspective is formed by folk tales, myths, religious scriptures, historical accounts, literature and erotic art, all of which permeate into the everyday practice of people. Every society has its own stores of such tales and myths, religious beliefs and traditions, which set the stage for everyday actions and experiences of sexual behaviour. In the Hindu perception of the divine, goddesses occupy an important place. In Nepal, this belief system is strongly influenced by Hinduism and to a considerable extent by *Tantric* Buddhism and shamanism. These three dimensions converge and intersect at several levels. In the predominant mythological tradition, male and female principles combine to make a single cosmic reality. In this reality, female sexuality represents the half but active principle of the Universe. She embodies fertility, fecundity and all the creative energies of the cosmos. The other half is the male half. These traditions are loaded with an abundance of sexual imagery and symbolism, culminating in the message of creative principles and duality merging into one reality—the paradoxical unity.

Relationship between Sexuality and Empowerment

Sexuality has deep implications for poverty alleviation, participation in society as well as democratic and human rights. One cannot imagine reproductive rights and gender equality without sexual rights. Recent studies have shown that sexual minorities (lesbians, gays, bisexuals, transgendered and intersex people) are discriminated against, often denied basic human and citizenship rights and are subjected to violence and exclusion. They face discrimination within the family, in school, in health services, in political participation, in the labour market and employment, and in all walks of society, economy and polity. If human rights are considered to be universal, indivisible and interdependent, sexual rights are also deeply embedded with the rights to education, health, employment, participation, mobility and equality.

Findings

Findings from the fieldwork and a review of secondary literature and surveys show that sex and sexuality remain taboos across most of Nepali society. The resulting reluctance to discuss these issues hinders the ability of women to negotiate a safe and pleasurable sexual experience and their lack of awareness and education concerning sex and sexuality leaves them vulnerable to exploitation, sexually transmitted diseases and early childbearing. In spite of several pieces of more progressive legislation emanating from the government, sexual minorities still face discrimination in society.

The Way Forward

Education, liberating sex and sexuality from their current 'dirty' and 'destructive' connotations, is an imperative step, which will allow for a more open and informed debate about these concepts and how they define, affect and influence the way people live their lives. Interventions, while remaining culturally informed and sensitive, must be widespread and part of a country-wide network of development and empowerment initiatives. Sexuality as a vital component of empowerment (of men as well as women and sexual minorities) needs to be acknowledged in development initiatives of the future.

1 | INTRODUCTION

Sexuality is a term defying a single definition or label, describing much more than one easily definable characteristic or trait. It refers to the entire way in which a person goes about expressing herself/himself as a sexual being, including innate attributes such as sexual desires, roles, identities and orientations. It represents a complex, rich and subtle world of experiences. What constitutes 'sexuality' can change with time and place. Sometimes elevated to the level of devotion, sometimes restricted to procreation and at other times desexualized, as in the case of the Bhakti movement[1] and erotic arts. Sometimes it is embodied in particular organs of body designated as 'sexual', while at other times it is disembodied, requiring no physical contact. As Menon says, different kinds of ideas, values and representations construct meshes which mould and label some acts as 'sex'. This mesh is historically and geographically fluid, leaving 'sex' not a clear and specific, physical and always recognizable phenomenon. As Menon (2007:xxviii) puts it:

> '... under different circumstances a "sexual" act can involve "non-sexual" parts of the body, such as arms or hands, or may not involve contact with the body at all, such as men exposing themselves to unknown women in public, or may be oral or verbal. We would agree that there are circumstances in which these kinds of performances too, could be identified as "sexual".'

According to the World Health Organization (WHO), sexuality 'is a central aspect of being human throughout life and encompasses sex, gender identities and roles, sexual orientation, eroticism, pleasure, intimacy and reproduction. Sexuality is experienced and expressed

---

[1] In Hinduism, *bhakti* describes the relation between the devotee and his/her personal god, which is characterized by intense mutual emotional attachment on the part of a devotee to his/her god. While *bhakti* as a religious path was already a central concept in the *Bhagavad Gita*, the Bhakti Movement was a rapid growth of *bhakti* from the 4th to the 18th centuries in South Asia, which began to impact all aspects of the Hindu culture.

in thoughts, fantasies, desires, beliefs, attitudes, values, behaviours, practices, roles and relationships. While sexuality can include all of these dimensions, not all of them are always experienced or expressed. Sexuality is influenced by the interaction of biological, psychological, social, economic, political, cultural, ethical, legal, historical and religious and spiritual factors' (WHO 2002). Thus, sexuality has several dimensions: relational, sensual, recreational, procreational, emotional, spiritual and physical. It is deeply embedded within wider issues of health, personal relationships and intimacies, economic and social well-being, equitable access to public services, freedoms and rights of men and women, girls and boys. Sexuality refers to the aspects of gender identity that relate to sex. As far as sexual behaviour is concerned, men in many societies can be proud of having multiple partners because it shows their sexual prowess. But for women, sex is predominantly about pleasing men (husbands) and about having babies. Hence, sexuality often refers to male needs and desires, while women's sexuality is looked down upon, ignored, feared and repressed. Jackson and Scott have aptly captured the multiple ways sexuality has been perceived and deployed historically:

> *'Sexuality is conventionally singled out as a special area of life: it has been variously romanticized and tabooed, seen as a threat to civilization, or the route to social revolution, as a source of degradation and a means to personal growth... Sexuality may be feared as a source of dirt, disease and degradation, but it is equally revered as a gateway to ecstasy, enlightenment and emancipation.' (Jackson and Scott, 1996:26)*

Representations of female sexuality date back to prehistoric times and the enactment of some form of norms to regulate the female body, and sexuality has been a characteristic of all major civilizations. For Will Durant, one of the core functions of civilization has been sexual regulation. According to him, the reproductive instinct creates problems not only within marriage but also before and after it, and threatens at any moment to disturb the social order with its persistence, intensity and possible perversions (Durant, 1935). Generally, women are regarded as symbols of charm, energy and fecundity. Isis in Egypt, Aphrodite in Greece, Venus in Rome and Ishtar in Babylon symbolized such prowess. Ishtar, in many ways, resembles the Mahashakti in Hindu traditions. Similarly, female sexuality has been perceived in patriarchal cultures throughout the world as threatening to order and social norms. Accordingly, it was considered necessary to subordinate women to male sexuality, and restrictions of various forms were placed on their behaviour through the application of what is called 'disciplinary technologies' and surveillance.

With a few exceptions, Nepal traditionally has been, and still continues to be, a predominantly patriarchal feudal society, with 'upper class and upper caste' men exercising power in the family, community and the state. In this tradition, men were considered free to move around and engage sexually with multiple partners, or to take more than one wife, while the institution of marriage was created to ensure female monogamy. In a feudal patriarchal society—and arguably in many of today's capitalist systems, a woman's body and sexuality are treated essentially as commodities, with primary duties of pleasing her husband and bearing children. Her failure to do so can result in her rejection from the family as well as physical and emotional torture from both her family and society. The traditional Nepali society constructed and enforced behavioural norms for women, which emphasized the suppressing of sexuality and prescribing codes for keeping their bodies under surveillance. The central goal of such norms was to instil modesty, chastity and fidelity in women and to instruct them to devote themselves with body and soul to one man. The purpose was essentially the controlling of women's sexuality, while similar controls were not placed on men. Women violating such norms caused their families, in-laws and kin dishonour, embarrassment and shame. Virginity and chastity were valued above all other qualities in women. In fact, sexual subjugation and control of women was and is the prime cause of their disempowerment in multiple dimensions of their lives.

As sexuality is generally considered a taboo and existing only in the private domain in Nepali society, it is not discussed openly. Information on this subject is tightly guarded. From all impressions, it appears that the issue of sexuality in Nepal is approached from a perspective of established stereotypes and received notions of the accepted positions of women and men in a patriarchal society. These represent the uniformity and linearity of the discourse and practices. Available information and evidence concerning the various dimensions of sexuality is scarce and fragmented. No systematic mapping of the arena has been accomplished so far. Neither have the relations of sexuality with the issues of women's empowerment been looked at in a convincing way.

In Nepal's context, a cursory examination of recent discourse indicates that women's empowerment has been understood and practised only in terms of upgrading women's social and economic status and, more recently, in equal representation of women in governmental bodies. The link between sexuality and empowerment has so far been understood only at a superficial level. It has been approached from religious, patriarchal and biomedical perspectives, and has been primarily concerned with safe motherhood, HIV/AIDS and reproductive rights.

Gender activists working with poor women have so far tended to see only economic and social discriminations and poverty as being critical issues. Hence, these strategies have remained focused only on social, economic and political empowerment, and little thought has been given to the connections between sexuality and women's empowerment and development. It is essential to make the people and larger society realize that female sexuality should be respected and women should have control over their own bodies and sexuality, free of coercion, discrimination and violence. It is time to realize that the perceptions and practices of sexuality have been some of the major causes of gender-based violence in Nepal.

Rationale of Study

It is high time the debate on the body as well as sexuality was promoted and policy relevant information on various aspects of sexuality in general and women's sexuality in particular in the context of Nepali society was generated. The time has come for women's sexuality and sexual expression to be considered integral parts of their lives and a central feature of their empowerment process. Globally, as well as in South Asia, sexuality discourses have already made pathways in the face of resurging religious fundamentalism, increased militarization, spread of HIV and AIDS and the persistent preference for male children. There is an ongoing debate highlighting the rights of women to control their lives and sexualities. Against this backdrop, Nepal also needs to look into the empowering and liberating possibilities of this discourse in the context of 'New Nepal'. It is necessary to deploy this discourse to expand the freedom of women and sexual minorities and to unmask the unfair distinctions, discriminations and violence faced by those not conforming to gender and sexual norms across a range of expressions, behaviours and identities. The first step towards this end could be to carry out a situation analysis of such expressions, behaviours and identities vis-à-vis social norms and state policies.

With that end in mind, Shtrii Shakti (S2) carried out this study. This study has its own limitations, but, on the whole, it is expected to break the silence surrounding sexuality and to promote discourse on the topic. In fact, S2 has already been implementing programmes geared towards the awakening and empowering of women in need. It has been involved in providing knowledge, attitudes and skills for women, along with efforts towards capacity building, networking and advocacy. Drawing on past experience, we now believe it is critical to move into the realm of sexuality to further the struggle of women's empowerment. This study is expected to equip S2 with information about the current situation in the country, which will eventually help it design or improve its training manuals from the perspective of sexuality education and women's empowerment.

Objectives

The study was designed and carried out with the following specific objectives in mind:

1. To break the silence around the issues of sexuality in the community and improve opportunities for open discussion of sexuality-based issues.
2. To look at sexuality from different dimensions, especially from an empowerment perspective, in relation to gender.
3. To educate teachers, community leaders, women and men, and to change public opinion on sexuality and on respecting the sexuality of women.
4. To disseminate knowledge and understanding and increase access to information and services concerning sexuality in the community
5. To enhance the capacities of existing gender, reproductive health and informal education trainers in relation to sexuality.
6. To provide policy recommendations on issues of female sexuality.

Methodology

This situation analysis is mainly based on a desk review of secondary sources of information. Theoretical discourses and relevant surveys are used to the extent available. Sexuality being a relatively new topic, not much data was available. Field work was done in the areas of three village development committees (VDCs) in Baglung district, Lekhani, Bhimpokhara and Bhiun, where impressions were collected from the grass roots level.

Limitations of the Study

As systematic and comprehensive empirical studies on sexuality have not been done in the past, this report has had to rely on scarce information collected from diverse sources. Much of the available information was not prepared from the perspective of sexuality and, accordingly, had limited use. Again, due to the diverse regional, ethnic, religious and other background characteristics of the population, the available information may not capture their subtle uniqueness and experiences. Given the ambition of the project, its primary data frame was also less than adequate. The complex and elusive character of sexuality itself made the task of crystallizing a theme difficult. These limitations have all made their impressions in this report.

Organization of the Report

This report is organized into four chapters. The first chapter has introduced sexuality, set the context, and outlined the objectives, methods and limitations of the study. The second chapter reviews theories, approaches and perspectives concerning sexuality. It also tries to look into the relationship between sexuality and empowerment. The third chapter tries to map out understanding and practices of sexuality in the Nepali context by relying on various sources. The last chapter tries to sum up findings from the situation analysis and put forward some recommendations for future work.

2 | THEORIES, APPROACHES AND PERSPECTIVES

Background

Historically, almost all major civilizations have developed their own codes and institutions for the regulation of sexuality, sexual relations and women's bodies. All civilizations considered this necessary as women or their sexuality could be a perennial source of conflict, violence and possible societal degeneration (Durant, 1935:36). The most universal and basic form of such regulation has been marriage.

Primitive men and women experienced every conceivable form of relations. In sum, the sexual codes in primitive society were very liberal and permissive. Sometimes tribes lived in 'marriageless' associations, where men and women were 'freer than birds', as in Borneo (Durant, 1935). In primitive Russia, women lived without appointed husbands. Native Americans, Papuans of New Guinea, Soyots of Siberia, Igorots of the Philippines, natives of Upper Burma and Siam, Bushmen of Africa, and certain tribes of Nigeria, Uganda, the Murray Islands and Polynesia practised very liberal attitudes towards premarital sexual relations and promiscuity. In many communities, premarital pregnancy was not an impediment to finding a husband. In Tibet and Malabar, virgin girls had difficulty in finding husbands (ibid: 45). In certain tribes in the Philippines, men were hired to end the virginity of prospective brides (ibid: 46). Accordingly, the importance given to chastity and virginity was a later development; primitive men dreaded not the loss of virginity but sterility. In sum, the sexual codes in primitive society were very liberal and permissive.

It appears that primitive societies were matrilineal and children's descent was traced through the mother. The earliest form of divinity worshipped by human beings was the Mother Goddess, which was inspired by the woman's power of giving birth and nurturing life. In prehistoric Europe, she was worshipped as the Crowned Butterfly Goddess (Crete) and Bird Goddess (Spain). She was called, in parts of Africa Ala, Anansi and Bahuba, in Latin America Chicomecoatl and Coatlicue, in Egypt Auset and Aniket, in other parts of the Middle East Al-Uzza, Arianna, Anuket and Hathor, in Greece Isis, Demeter, Gaea, Galatea, in India and Tibet Kundalini, Bhavani, Kali, Chomo Lung-ma and Khon-ma, in China Mat Chinoi and Kwan Yin, and in North America Awitelin Tsita and Butterfly Women. All are depicted as life-giving divine figures with exaggeratedly huge breasts and bellies (Batliwala, 2006). In fact, in all early civilizations women were revered and their sexuality celebrated.

The search for virginity, chastity, marital fidelity and devotion was mainly the result of the emergence of the institution of private property, as men sought to ensure that their own blood inherited their hard-earned fortunes. As only women could know the father of her child, it led to an insistence on premarital chastity and post-marital fidelity among women. Among men, the only way to ensure that children were their own biological offspring was to restrict the sexuality of women by controlling their freedom of movement, their access to, and interaction with, other men, their independent ownership of resources and other freedoms they had enjoyed so far. At the same time, no such restrictions were placed on men, who could be engaged sexually with multiple partners. Other historical events, such as the advent of war and slavery, also facilitated women's subordination (Batliwala, 2006).

Initially, control over women's autonomy and sexual freedom was imposed through force. Over time, subtler control mechanisms of social mores, cultural norms and religious doctrines were developed, along with sanctions for violators. The institution of marriage, emphasis on female monogamy, the creation of the categories 'good women' and 'bad women' and their respective attributes, and an increased importance on virginity and sexual chastity all combined to ensure women's subordination. Consequently, women themselves became the agents of their own subordination by teaching and perpetuating patriarchal norms, enforcing compliance, and policing and punishing deviance. Thus, a whole set of institutions, cultural values and norms was constructed and deployed around women's sexuality. Women's mobility was strictly controlled, especially before and during their reproductive age, and those violating these norms were considered 'bad women', whores and harlots. Ideas of sex and sexuality were rendered taboo. Parts of the body associated with sex and reproduction were labelled 'polluting' and tainted organs, to be ashamed of, to be hidden, shunned and abhorred. Sexual desires were something to be feared. Even though not always explicitly expressed, women are often depicted as inherently wanton, promiscuous and incapable of controlling their desires; hence, the need for strict control (Batliwala, 2006). These processes in different cultures and locations around the world gathered momentum over the centuries to make subordination of women complete to the extent that, in some areas, women were made to join their dead husbands on their funeral pyres as *satis*[2]. Heterosexuality was accepted as the dominant and 'natural' norm, and all other sexual practices were rendered abnormal and thereby pathologized.[3] Over time, the whole subject of sex and sexuality was tabooed, kept confined in the darkrooms of the night and information about it tightly guarded.

Evidently, women did not give up easily. The struggle in one form or another, sometimes manifest and latent and at other times embedded within overarching power relations, continues to impress the relations between men and women and husband and wife. At times strong rivalries and conflicts are perceived between spouses both within and without the household, and even Indian mythologies reflect such debates and struggles concerning male and female superiority among deities and demons (Kakar, 2007:14).

Winds of Change

In spite of the taboos associated with the subject, sexual practices and identities have attracted growing attention from researchers and clinicians in the biological, psychological and social sciences. Sexual instincts, reproductive processes, venereal diseases, man-woman relations and variations in practices continue to keep scholars engaged. In the post-war period, lesbian and gay civil rights movements began to gather momentum. From the 1970s onwards, sexual practices and identities became major topics of academic, political and cultural debate in the USA. Several rights movements, including those of sexual minorities, began to undermine long-established moral principles and challenge the

---

[2] *Sati* was a Hindu ritual in which wife of a dead husband was burnt on his funeral pyre in few cases on her own choice and in most cases coerced.

[3] This term is used to describe a process by which unacceptable sexual practices were rendered as a kind of sickness or pathology.

dominant notions of sex and sexuality. Particularly, women's movements, rising divorce rates, widespread use of sexual imagery in advertising and television programmes, and the increasing visibility of sexual minorities all pointed to the decline of traditional ideals of gender and sexuality. Similarly, of late, technological advances have opened up the debate of sexuality in new arenas. The practices of vitro-fertilization, surrogate motherhood and surgical assignment of gender raised new legal issues. Transgender activists and others who did not conform to gender norms continued their struggle for the recognition of their rights. Growing feminist scholarships, human rights conventions (particularly CEDAW and consecutive women's conferences) nurtured and supported the varying movements striving for the protection of the human rights of women and sexual minorities and supported gender mainstreaming in development processes.

For centuries, South Asian societies have had the distinction of being very conservative from the perspective of sexuality. Generally, sex and sexuality are considered to be 'dirty topics' and people avoid talking about them. Those who are vocal about sex-related issues are considered less cultured and even immoral. People silently suffer varying kinds of depression, unhappiness and other complex physical and psychological problems. No systematic studies or research are encouraged. For a worryingly large section of society, things like premarital sex and HIV are imports from the West and are bad cultural influences. Even couples do not discuss sexual matters. People prefer to believe that problems come from outside the country and forget that we share the same desires and feelings. Same sex relations are regarded as a perversion and social evil, and people in same sex relationships are often subject to prejudices and discrimination. A number of misconceptions concerning various sexual and health issues exist.

The winds of change have reached different parts of the world, including South Asia. In the South Asian context, women's empowerment has generally been equated with strategies that improve women's social, economic and political power and autonomy and with enhancing women's self-esteem and participation in decision-making in a number of spheres. Another concern is with increasing women's access to resources, challenging the gender biases within social, economic and political structures and in institutions like the family, education and the media. These empowerment programmes have highlighted the ideology of patriarchy or male domination, which has subordinated and subjugated women but have not embraced the link with sexuality in either concept or practice and still exhibit a deep discomfort, awkwardness and escapist attitude towards the subject of sexuality. Accordingly, this issue was nowhere to be seen in the development discourse until the HIV/AIDS pandemic hit the subcontinent (Batliwala, 2006).

Some have resented the discourses on sexuality as the product of corrupting western influence, while others argue that the activists are mechanically trying to imitate western experience in this part of the world. To these one activist replies:

> '... we do not repeat what happened in the West—it is not a linear movement—the context is different, the issues are different. We are not behind them—our context makes things happen. The scales, the scope of the dialogue are quite different from what happened in the West a few decades ago. In the West it was about individualism and lifestyle; it is more about cultural and political issues as well as rights on a larger scale.' (Thu-Hong, 2006)

During the last ten to fifteen years, people and media in South Asia have become more open about topics like premarital sex, divorce and same sex relations. Campaigns focusing on human rights, sexual and reproductive health, HIV/AIDS and sexual and domestic violence have brought the issue of sexuality out of the private realm. Tolerance of a wide range of sexual expressions has increased, and respect for sexual diversity in the institutions of the state, civil societies and religious establishments is on the rise. Improvements have been made in the delivery of sexual and reproductive health services. However, only limited success has been achieved in linking gender and sexuality issues with human rights. Sexuality is still surrounded by visible and invisible inhibitions, dark secrets, stigmas and discriminations, which can all have severe effects on the quality of life and place constraints on sexual practices and expressions. Non-conformists face sanctions and penalties ranging from ostracism and discrimination to violence. The decisions taken by various legal systems, the police, employers and healthcare services are frequently influenced by issues of gender and sexuality and in some cases, such as the criminalization of same sex preference, people not conforming to traditional gender and sexual norms can be discriminated against (Misra and Chandiramani, 2007).

The women's rights movement has brought about changes in women's access to education, employment and political office, as well as in their sexual lives. This was the result of their concerted efforts at various levels, ie advocacy, lobbying and mobilization. The global flow of information and the role of the media have increased, and activism by national and international activists has promoted the acceptance of single women having sexual relationships, couples living outside traditional marriage and same sex behaviour in different parts of the world (Misra and Chandiramani, 2007). Research is being carried out on different aspects of sexuality, but much has yet to be done concerning sexual lives, practices, knowledge, beliefs and concepts about sexuality and the way it changes over time.

Born out of the women's movements and women's studies, the men's movements and men's studies have emerged to add strength to these winds of change. Recognizing that men have their own sex and gender (as opposed to assuming a male perspective was universal, as reflected in such terms as 'the family of man or mankind'), scholars of men's studies and activists have begun to develop a body of research and set of initiatives to act as allies to not only create changes in women's rights, but also to urge men to face up to issues such as domestic abuse or gender-based violence and liberate themselves from constricting sex and gender roles that lead to dramatically shorter life expectancies and global problems.

Perspectives

Sexuality is a contested topic and is construed differently in different parts of the world at different times. The politics of knowledge is also intense in this arena as it remains a site where power is played out. It is not possible to trace here the genealogy of the discourse and practise of sexuality across the diverse local cultural traditions; neither is it possible to map out the real historical processes and negotiations through which a certain version of sexuality was 'normalized' by a society. No historical literature is available other than the very recent efforts to deal with the issues of sexual minorities. There have been efforts to approach the issue of sexuality from different perspectives. A brief review of some of these approaches is in order:

Anthropological Perspective

For anthropologists, particular versions of sexual practices, sexual identities and orientations are the impressions of a surrounding society, its way of life, norms and belief systems. Emphasis is placed on the role of culture and learning in shaping sexual behaviours and attitudes, and universalism and essentialism are rejected. Although 'sexual drive' is biologically determined and almost universal, culture can encourage or discourage sexual expressions and acts, attitudes and relationships. Certain practices are accepted in certain societies and cultures, whereas certain acts are not. Therefore, human actions, including sexual acts, are subject to historical and cultural forces. The body, its functions, sensations, potentials and limits are all mediated by the surrounding culture (Vance, 1999:46).

Accordingly, while studying sexuality, anthropologists look into the social structure, economic organization, norms, values and belief systems, taboos and rituals, power relations and codes of behaviour, as well as sexual division of labour, among the population. Sex, sexuality, pleasure and social control are all shaped by encompassing social systems. Historically, different societies have evolved their own codes of behaviour and practices as dictated by their own requirements and values (Abbott et al., 2005:229). Among many cultures, female sexuality is considered to be subordinate to male sexuality. In ancient Indian society, for instance, women's sexuality was controlled through practices such as child marriage, prohibition of widow remarriage and *sati*. Similarly, it was suppressed by withholding sexual information, instilling a fear of pregnancy and of men, as well as creating a sense of shame in relation to one's body and sexuality among girls. Muslim women are symbolically represented through a veil that covers their head in a headscarf or cloaks the body from head to toe. Some interpretations of Islam forbid women from leaving the seclusion of the home, and, if she must enter the public sphere, she must be fully veiled so that no part of her body is exposed. As sexuality is a subtle experience and not easily understood through a cursory study, the ethnographic and participant observation techniques often employed by anthropologists are considered to be appropriate for such matters.

Feminist Perspective

Feminism, with its ideal of the common sisterhood of all women, embraced a unitary and 'emancipatory' politics. The analysis of power relations is central to a feminist perspective of the nature and causes of women's subordination. Drawing on the traditional concept of power as a repressive force, they have sought to explain women's oppression by patriarchal social structures and ideological underpinnings. Though feminists make a distinction between gender and sexuality, they believe that one cannot be understood properly without reference to the other. They also believe that sexuality is embedded in power relations, which are in turn influenced by gender relations. Sexuality has been a central theoretical and political issue for feminists and also a source of major divisions. According to Valarie Bryson (2003:187), existing sexual behaviour is neither natural nor freely chosen, but closely tied up with the notions of ownership, domination and submission.

There is diversity within feminist scholarship with regard to sexuality and sexual rights. Radical feminists emphasize that ultimately it is men who abuse, harass and rape women and who buy and use pornography and commercial sex. Women's subordination is perpetuated primarily through men's control over their bodies and sexuality. Just as the exploitation of labour is at the heart of class relations, so is sexual exploitation fundamental to the 'sex class system'. Therefore, feminists emphasize sexual autonomy and fulfilment as part of the general political struggle against patriarchy. Anne Koedt, in her *The Myth of the Vaginal Orgasm*, argues that female sexual pleasure, being located in the clitoris, does not require penile penetration. This led to the demand for the 'right to orgasm' and towards renegotiating sexual practise with male partners. For Marxists and socialists, the pursuit of orgasm can be an important political issue only for middle class white women or the bourgeois. For women involved in a struggle for basic economic survival, it does not have much appeal.

Pornography provides one example of the exploitation of women. It degrades and abuses women by eroticizing men's power over women and promotes violence against women. Historically, enormous efforts, from chastity belts to property laws, have been made to control female sexuality and to tie women to individual men through monogamous heterosexual relationship. Feminists stand against the objectification of women in beauty contests, advertisements and prostitution. Many are critical of the sexual revolution and many aspects of the so-called 'sexual liberation', which for them is simply an 'eroticization of women's oppression'. Whether heterosexuality is a tenable practice for feminists remains at the centre of the debate. They also emphasize that heterosexuality does not have the same meaning for all men and women. Heterosexuality, which is considered to be a natural drive or social choice, is in fact imposed on women, and is institutionalized through law, education, religion and language. Feminists have seen heterosexuality as an institution through which men have appropriated women's bodies and labour. Heterosexual activity has always been risky for women and associated with 'loss of reputation', unwanted pregnancy and diseases which threaten fertility. Lesbianism, for many of them, is a form of resistance against patriarchal power and an alternative to heteronormativity (Abbott et al., 2005). The idea of the family as the natural and normal site of sexual relations privileges heterosexuality and renders deviant any sexual relations outside its norm.

Similarly, women's accounts of sexual pleasure during heterosexual relations and media images of women as sexual beings are largely labelled male sexual fantasies, which intimate a continuous lack of sexual agency among young women. In all depictions, they are portrayed as recipients or victims and not as initiators of sexual encounters. Girls who are conscious of their sexual desire are also under pressure to contain it. However, in real life experiences, women have developed their own ways and strategies to disrupt the heterosexual norms, though not always without considerable risk of family and social sanctions. But these are individual strategies and not collective acts of resistance. More libertarian feminists argue that any form of censorship is socially undesirable and works against the interests of women. Others believe that a preoccupation with pornography and sexuality deflects attention from more fundamental feminist issues. In any case, sexuality has been central to feminist theory and politics. In contrast to the strident feminist, the post-feminist is viewed as fun-loving, sexy and independent. She is indifferent to, or even critical of, politics and not very enthusiastic about solidarity with other women for liberation, and she is 'far too busy having an orgasm to worry about such issues'. The post-feminist woman is a 'free agent' beyond any definition or label, free of allegiances and with a sense of empowered sexuality. She represents a bad girl image; her body is a glamorous object over which she has a complete control (Tarrier, 2005). Post-feminism claims to be transgressive and emphasizes the 'marginal' and the 'subversive', as well as a radical departure from the feminist monolith in both the academic arena and popular culture.

Thus, feminism is not a monolith but a series of diverse movements. The differences in theoretical basis and practical approach and the division of feminists into radical, separatist, libertine and other strands weakened the feminist movement from within (Abbott et al., 2005:212). In fact, the tension between heterosexuality and lesbianism disrupted any progress made towards a unified movement. However, there are some others who take a less disruptive line by trying to engage themselves and encourage others to engage productively in theorizing the diverse sexual experiences and attitudes of women. Sexual violence has been one of the major concerns of feminists and a key focus of their political activities.

Biomedical Perspective

Conventionally, the issue of sexuality has mostly been dealt with from the biomedical perspective. The biomedical approach considers sexuality as a pre-social biological entity. It tends to reduce women's sexuality to physiological characteristics and organic and reproductive processes, and dissociates the individual from the 'body'. A biomedical perspective also tends to downplay the fact that sexuality has a history and its definitions and meanings change over time between and within populations. It focuses on understanding a woman's body through an anatomical and physiological lens and talks about reproductive organs and processes. Age, hormone level, specific illnesses and malfunctioning body parts are its concerns, which are diagnosed and treated using prescribed methods. Sexual orientation, expressions and behaviours are attributed to a genetic predisposition that is biologically determined. The medical profession takes a woman's body as a patient and gives instructions about aspects of personal hygiene and physiological well-being, which excludes intimate bodily experiences. With the ascendancy of social construction and discursive theories, its authority has to some extent declined. However, with the spread of HIV/AIDS, there has been a resurgence of the biomedical approach to sexuality and the medicalization of sexuality is intensifying as the public turns to medical authorities for sexual information and advice (Vance, 1999:47). Sexual and reproductive health usually focuses on physiological characteristics, organic and reproductive processes and diseases such as STDs and HIV/AIDS, ignoring the complex gender power relations and pleasures which the sexual activity involves (Holland et al., 1994). As sexual well-being is increasingly being felt to be a function of gender relations, as well as an important part of general well-being, the biomedical approach is becoming increasingly inadequate to address the issues of women's sexual rights and empowerment.

Social Construction Theory

This approach stands almost in contrast to the biomedical approach. It puts less emphasis on the biological aspects of sex, body and sexuality. According to this approach, sexuality is a social construction that is discursively produced as an instrument of social and political control. The main proponent of this approach is Michel Foucault (1977, 1979). According to him, in modern society, the behaviour of individuals and groups is controlled by establishing standards of normality, which are disseminated through a range of 'scientific administrative discourses' such as criminology, medicine, psychology and psychiatry, which generate and claim 'truth'. The eighteenth and nineteenth centuries tended to understand sex as a biological and psychic drive with deep links to identity. Discourses went on to spell out the normal and healthy as well as the perverted and pathological forms of sexual behaviour. Once the categories and scale of 'normal' and 'pathological' were established, political technologies for treating and reforming deviant or pathological behaviour were deployed. This is all accomplished so skilfully and efficiently that modern individuals and social groups themselves become the agents of their own normalization and surveillance. Consequently, they become self-regulating normalized individuals requiring less and less external enforcement. Judith Butler believes that the seemingly natural masculine gender and heterosexual desire in male bodies is culturally constructed through the repetition of stylized acts over time. Accordingly, for her, all three categories of sex, gender and sexuality are 'performative'. However, the performance is not voluntary but confined to spaces created by 'regulative discourses', which in advance determine the possibility of performance (Butler, 1993, 1999).

Foucault believes that the body is the principal site of power and control in modern society. Women's bodies, minds and sexuality have been prime objects of control and normalization. They are subjected to disciplinary practices such as dieting, exercise and beauty regimens to conform to the prevailing patriarchal norms of feminine identity, namely beauty and attractiveness. These disciplinary technologies are particularly effective as they work at the level of body, gestures, desires and habits. In his *History of Sexuality*, Foucault analyses the production of the category of sex and the way it was deployed by regimes to control the sexual body and also the way in which the productive operations of power are disguised under the 'natural' sex functions. Here, sexuality is represented as an unruly natural drive which should be repressed and disciplined. He emphasizes the contingent and socially determined nature of sexuality and, thereby, frees the body of the regulatory fiction of heterosexuality and opens up new realms in which bodily pleasures can be explored (McNay, 1992:32).

Foucault's idea of body and sexuality as cultural constructs rather than natural phenomena is refreshing. He challenges the commonly-held notion of power as an essentially negative and repressive force operating purely through the mechanisms of law, taboo and censorship. For him, power, which is productive and constitutive, creates the domains of normalized practices and phenomena. Hence, he claims that modern regimes of power operate to produce us as subjects who are both objects and vehicles of power. This view of power assumes that power is exercised rather than possessed, it is evolving rather than fixed, it is constitutive rather than imposed from outside or above. It does not emanate from the top, but circulates throughout the social body, constantly working and reworking the social relations. There is a mutually reinforcing relation between knowledge (scientific technical discourses) and 'productive' power.

From the seventeenth century onwards, when the growth and care of its population increasingly became the primary concern of the state, new mechanisms of power emerged. These new forms of bio-power had two dimensions. The first was efficient government of the population through management of the life processes of the social body. It involved the regulation of birth, death, sickness, disease, health and sexual relations. The second was cultivation of 'disciplinary power', targeting the human body as the object of manipulation and training. Disciplinary power subjects bodily activities to constant surveillance and examination. The aim is to optimize the body's capacities, skills, usefulness and productivity through calculated manipulation of its elements, gestures and behaviour. Thus, the human body is made subject to the mechanics of power, which explore, break down and reassemble it. Discipline produces subjected and practised bodies, the 'docile bodies' (Foucault, 1977:138-39). The instrument of disciplinary power and constant surveillance is initially geared towards disciplining the body, gradually takes hold of the mind, and a psychological state of permanent visibility (ibid) ensues as perpetual surveillance is internalized by individuals. According to Foucault, a transition to modernity entails the replacement of law by the norm as the primary instrument of social control.

Foucault tries to show that, in the eighteenth and nineteenth centuries, sex and sexuality became crucial political issues in the course of managing the lives of the population. This was intimately connected with the social science discourses on sex and sexuality. These discourses tended to understand sex as an instinctual, biological and psychic drive with potentially far-reaching effects on the social behaviour of individuals. The idea that sexual drive could function in a healthy and normal way, as well as in a perverse or pathological way, led to the classification of behaviour along the scale of normalization and pathologization. Once the social categories of normal and pathological were established, efforts were made to maximize normal and treat deviant behaviour 'in the interest of both individual and society'. For Foucault, truth is relative and political in nature. This also means that the institutions of marriage, motherhood and compulsory heterosexuality are deeply gendered and power-laden.

Mythological Perspective

This perspective is formed by folk tales, myths, religious scriptures, historical accounts, literature, art and the everyday practices of people. Every society has its own system of tales and myths, religious beliefs and traditions, which set the stage for everyday actions and experience of life. Goddesses occupy an important place in the Hindu perception of the divine. In Nepal, this belief system is strongly influenced by Hinduism and to a considerable extent by *Tantric* Buddhism and shamanism. These three dimensions converge and intersect at several levels. In the predominant mythological tradition, male and female principles combine to make a single cosmic reality. In this reality, female sexuality represents the active principle of the Universe. She embodies fertility, fecundity and all the creative energies of cosmos. The other half is the male half. These traditions are loaded with an abundance of sexual imagery and symbolism.

According to the *Shakta*[4] tradition of Hinduism, the governing principle of the universe is 'the female' *Shakti*, which, in a sense, is God as Mother. The entire universe emanates from her womb. *Shakti*, the embodiment of primeval energy, conceives, bears, produces and nourishes all worlds and species. Time and space, as well as all that are therein, are her manifestations. Supreme Brahman, though the Cause of all causes, is ever-existent, unchanging, omnipresent, pure intelligence and all

---

[4] *Shakta* is the follower/worshipper of Shakti, a religious path.

encompassing, acts not and moves not. So, it is the Mahashakti moved by His desire who creates, protects and destroys this world. There are a number of goddesses who are embodiments of Mahashakti in *Tantric* Hinduism. Ten Mahavidyas (Kali, Tara, Tripurasundari, Bhuvaneswori, Chhinnamasta, Bhairavi, Dhumavati, Bagalamukhi, Matangi and Kamala) represent her different manifestations. Mahavidya iconography, mythology, worships and rituals are dominated by implicit and explicit sexual symbolism. Sexual intercourse is explicitly portrayed in *dhyana* (meditation) *mantras,* and the portraits of Kali, Chhinnamasta, Tara and most of the individual Mahavidyas are depicted as sexually attractive (Kinsley, 1998:141). The *yantras* that represent Mahavidyas contain implicit sexual symbols, and the central metaphor of awakening (*Kundalini Shakti*) itself can be understood as the arousal of sexual energy. This imagery reflects the *tantric* vision of reality as the dynamic interaction and tension between the two great principles, Shiva and Shakti (ibid:141).

According to the *Shankhya* philosophy, before all there is *Prakriti,* the primeval matter, Nature, which stands in contrast to *Purush,* the male principle. Without *Prakriti, Purush* is inert and inactive. These imageries permeate all the belief systems and practices in Hinduism. According to the *Tantras,* in the *shatkona,* or hexagon, which is so central to Hindu symbolism, the triangle represents three worlds and three *gunas*—the neutral, positive and the negative. In the *shatkona,* the triangle with its apex downwards represents *yoni,* the female organ of Shakti, the female energy or nature. The triangle which points upwards is the male principle, or *Purush.* When two triangles overlap each other, the creation of universe is symbolized. The superimposition of one triangle on the other symbolizes the union of Shiva and Shakti, which manifests itself in the creation of the universe.

Mythologically, Shakti is conceived as the spouse of Shiva and Shiva is the *Purush.* In fact, the Hindu mind is accustomed to seeing unity in multiplicity; so, a belief in Devi or Mahashakti embodies all gods and their energies. Brahma, Vishnu and Mahesh and their energies unite in her. She is the primordial Kali, Mahayogini.

As the highest deity is female, every woman is regarded as the embodiment of Devi. This conception has led many *tantric sadhakas* to woman worship. So potent is this *tantric* practice that the literature is filled with warnings and often a description of two paths to female worship. The right-hand path engages the *sadhaka* in a symbolic worship without actually engaging in sexual acts. The *Bammargis* (followers of the left-hand path) go to the extent of eating and offering meat, intoxicating themselves with wine, worshipping the *yoni* and engaging in sexual acts following elaborate ritual ceremonies (*Mantras, Yantras, Mudras* and *Nyasas*), which lead to wild orgies as the means to reach Her and come out in a purer, energized and nobler form. It is believed that, in *Kaliyug*, only one's own spouse should be enjoyed as Shakti.

A review of literature, some of which we have discussed above, provides us with insights into the female characters, energies or deities that are considered extraordinary treasures. This needs to be explored to give greater clarity to our new understanding or vision. Sexual embrace is particularly recommended for those of a passionate temperament, who tend to crave rather than abhor. Meditation sublimates craving and refines sexual energy. At the highest level, the two figures symbolize the union of wisdom (symbolized by Vajrayogini) and compassion (Heruka). Also, through deep inner concentration in *Tantric* meditation one can develop an intensely blissful state of mind and then use this to explore the nature of reality. So, Heruka and Vajrayogini also embody an enlightened state of consciousness in which Great Bliss is suffused with the understanding of emptiness.

Vassantara, in his book *Female Deities in Buddhism*, gives us a fascinating analysis of the feminine divine power. He examines female deities such as Tara (in Her multiple manifestations and forms) as queens, crones, Buddha goddesses, mothers, wild women and many other forms which inspire, beguile, rouse, protect and empower us. He invites readers, or seekers, to enter the magical realm of gently compassionate Kuan Yin from China, where the elusive golden the goddess from India, representing perfect wisdom, tangles with the energetic embodiments of freedom, the fearless sky-dancing *dakinis* of Tibet.

Manu, the Hindu lawgiver, demonstrates an ambiguous attitude towards women. On the one hand, he exalts women as goddesses of fortune and regards them as an integral part of rituals. He states: 'where women are honoured, there the gods are pleased, but where they are not honoured, no sacred rite yields reward.' Women are exalted in their maternal aspect as well. There is no difference between a wife who bears children and the goddess of fortune. However, his view of women as sexual beings is quite apprehensive. Her inner sexual proclivities are so dangerous that, according to him, a woman is never fit for independence and, therefore, should be protected by her father in childhood, by her husband in youth and by her sons in old age.

Before closing this section, it is important to note that there are new emerging perspectives from men's studies concerning traditional masculinities. According to Joseph Pleck, a lack of empowerment is experienced by many men as well. In what has come to be known as the 'Pleck paradox', the men he studied, who had power and control by virtue of their social position, were not aware of that power and actually lacked it. The social norms theory also shows the consistent misperceptions many men have of what is expected of them. While not agreeing with the traditional masculinity (described by James O'Neil as restricted emotionally, commitment to power or control, and conflict between work and leisure), men conform to this traditional masculine role because they think that is what other men expect of them. Men's studies attempt to expose the paradox and misperceptions many men labour under to address the issues articulated above. In this, men's studies may be seen to be closely allied with the beliefs and ideologies of some feminists.

Relationship between Sexuality and Empowerment

The relationship between sexuality and development goes largely unacknowledged in development literature. The issues of sex and sexuality, which constitute some of the most intimate experiences of human life, are associated with taboos, shame, stigmas and silence. Recently, it has begun to be acknowledged that sexuality has a deep impact on the livelihoods, security and well-being of people (Armas, 2007) and deep implications for poverty alleviation, participation in society, as well as upon democratic and human rights. One cannot imagine reproductive rights and gender equality without sexual rights. Sexuality, especially its 'normative' constructions, affects particularly those who do not conform to heteronormativity, and recent studies have shown that sexual minorities—lesbians, gays, bisexuals, transgendered and intersex people—are discriminated against, often denied basic human and citizenship rights, and are subjected to violence and exclusion. They face discrimination within the family, in school and health services, in political participation, the labour market, in employment and in all walks of society, economy and polity. Owing to obstacles and stigmas, they find it difficult to fully participate in social, political and economic life (ibid). Even people subscribing to heteronormativity, particularly women, are restricted in their mobility, denied a choice of partners, and subjected to coercive marital sex, unwanted pregnancy and STDs. In reality, very few people are fortunate enough to live out fulfilling, pleasurable and safe sexual relationships, free of coercion and violence.

Women and sexual minorities are particularly subject to 'symbolic mutilations' of desires, and are often stigmatized and forced to live with shame and guilt. As a result, they are excluded and ostracized by family and society, which has a direct bearing upon their mental health. All of these factors result in weaker capacities in varying public spheres and can lead to poverty. In fact, poverty, to a great extent, is a result of discrimination, exclusion and oppression. Without freedom, people cannot develop their capabilities and, without capacities, they cannot fight the forces that trap them into poverty.

Even in the discourses of gender equality, women's empowerment and reproductive health rights have sidelined sexuality—an issue so critical to the security and well-being of men, women and sexual minorities. The recent emphasis on human rights in international development has opened up opportunities to take on these issues of sexuality and particularly issues surrounding marginalized sexualities.

The Swedish government's definition of sexual rights states that all people, irrespective of sex, age, ethnicity, disability, gender identity or sexual orientation, have a right to their own body and sexuality. This qualification also encompasses the more general human rights principle of non-discrimination on sexual or any other grounds, such as sexual orientation and gender identity. According to WHO, sexual rights embrace human rights that are already recognized in national laws, international human rights documents and other consensus declarations. They include the right of all persons to:

- the highest attainable standard of sexual health, including access to sexual and reproductive healthcare services
- seek, receive and impart information related to sexuality
- sexuality education
- respect for bodily integrity

- choose their partner
- decide to be sexually active or not
- consensual sexual relations
- consensual marriage
- decide whether or not and when to have children, and
- pursue a satisfying, safe and pleasurable sexual life (cited in Armas, 2007).

If human rights are considered to be universal, indivisible and interdependent, sexual rights are also deeply embedded within the rights to education, health, employment, participation, mobility and equality. Accordingly, empowerment remains incomplete until women and sexual minorities are empowered to take charge of their bodies and sexuality.

Being a multicultural society, Nepal contains a wide variety of customs and values that impact sexuality and sexual encounters, and many variations are found across different caste or ethnic groups. However, patriarchy runs as the common thread across almost all social, cultural and religious groups. No comprehensive studies documenting the various aspects of sexuality found in the country have been carried out so far in the Nepali context. The only study that has partially covered aspects of sexuality is the National Demographic and Health Survey (NDHS). This survey focuses largely on the biomedical perspectives; information on other aspects is fragmentary and difficult to obtain. To some extent, the issue of sexuality in Nepal can be studied and analysed using the different theories and approaches discussed in Chapter II. The first section of this chapter deals with sexuality as part of the lifecycle of Nepali women.

3 | SEXUALITY IN NEPAL: UNDERSTANDING AND PRACTICES

General Attitude towards Girls and Women

The general attitude and behaviour towards women is characterized by ambivalence. On the one hand, women are regarded as goddesses representing a universal force, the Creative Principle, or Universal Mother. In the tradition of *Shakti* or *Devi*, a woman is regarded as the female counterpart of Shiva. She is *Prakriti*, the fertile female principle, providing the basis for the *Purush*. Shiva is powerful and active only with Shakti. The *Puranas* suggest that the trinity of Hinduism –Brahma, Bishnu and Shiva– all originated from the Original Mother, who finally took Shiva as her consort. In the *Tantric* tradition, Shakti has two main aspects: benevolent and terrifying. In the benevolent form, she is known as Gauri, Uma and Parvati, while in her dreadful form she is Durga, Kali, Chandi, Chamunda, Bhairavi and so on. A central belief of Hinduism in Nepal is that the active principle in the universe is feminine and that *Purusha*, or the male entity, is quiescent until it is energized by *Prakriti*, the female principle. These beliefs led to the association of women with power, vigour and energy. The whole universe is the emanation of Shakti; she is the creator, preserver and destroyer. From Shakti emerged the sixty-four *yoginis*, the energies of gods who were counterparts of the sixty-four forms of Bhairav. According to *tantrics*, without Shakti, or the female deity, gods are powerless. In Nepal, all forms of Shakti— Uma, Parvati, Kumari, Durga, Tara, Kali and so on—are worshipped. The *Tantrics* worship *yoni* as a goddess. The *Shakta* philosophy considers sexual union as the cosmic union of male and female principles. Shakti can be compared with *Kundalini* or the coiled or creative energy, the fundamental force of the cosmos (Majpuria). Goddesses are often depicted as charming women with seductive qualities, capable of casting *maya* even on gods. These qualities are praised in goddesses.

On the other hand, women in their human form are considered dangerous, and their charm and seductiveness are feared. Based on traditional beliefs, women are portrayed as inherently seductive, promiscuous, unfaithful, passionate, dangerously enticing and lacking sexual morality. There is a consistent fear of women as sexual beings and their potential to disrupt family and social harmony. Even within marriage, this view is so entrenched that traditionally a woman is not allowed to touch the father or brothers of her husband. A woman's sexuality is considered to be a restive and unruly force that makes her both dangerous and vulnerable. Accordingly, she must be subjected to a range of technologies of control. Some of these technologies emanate from entrenched patriarchy, while others come from religious discourses and ritual performances. The whole social order, with its accompanying institutions and socio-economic and cultural norms which govern the lives of Brahmin, Chhetri, Newar and certain Dalit women, appears, to a great extent, to be geared towards the regulation of their sexual relations.

Attitudes and behaviour towards women do not remain the same throughout a woman's life. As a daughter, she is treated as (and expected to be) a virgin in the house of her parents. Virginity is elevated and, therefore, a virgin daughter is revered and even worshipped at times. At the same time, she is also discriminated against as someone who will leave the house to join her future husband and in-laws. For many years in her new house, she remains an 'outsider', trying to overcome the undefined 'otherness' and, in many cases, open hostility on the part of her in-laws. She has to undergo all sorts of scrutiny and tests as a wife. Her behaviour in general and sexual behaviour in particular are closely monitored not only within the household but also in the wider community. Any deviation can be damaging to her conjugal life. When she becomes a revered mother or mother-in-law, her role and status is again enhanced. She commands respect and authority. Widowhood also has different impacts on mothers and daughters-in-law. It is more difficult for a daughter-in-law, while it is less so for a mother-in-law. In the following section, a brief sketch is presented of how a woman experiences her sexuality in Nepali society through different phases of her lifecycle.

As a Virgin Girl

The issue of sexuality is central to the lives of women and pervades throughout childhood, puberty, family relations, friendship, marriage, motherhood and the entire socialization process. Among Brahmins, Chhetris and Newars, virginity is valued and worshipped. A virgin girl, or *kanya* is considered to be pure (*aksheta*), unpolluted and auspicious. She is a goddess representing bounty, fertility, creative energy and prosperity.

Virginity is so valued in Hindu communities that, if a girl is known to have lost her virginity, she would find it difficult to get married. This has been the main cause of child marriage historically and continues to be practised among certain communities, particularly in the Terai.

The concept of *Kumari* is so central to traditional Newar communities in Kathmandu that every girl-child is thought of as an eternal virgin and a personification of the mother goddess herself. To attain this eternity, each girl-child is first married to a *bilva* fruit, symbolizing Lord Shiva Himself. In this wedding ceremony, known as *ihee*, all the rituals are aimed at ensuring that the girl remains fecund forever. The same girl, before marrying a man, is again wedded to another symbol of eternity, the Sun.[5] It is only after these two marriages that the girl is considered eligible to marry the earthly man. For Newars she represents the Good Earth of Kathmandu, embodying the female principle and eternal motherhood (Shrestha, 1997). The girl also represents all the feminine principles ranging from innocence, purity and virginity to the seductive charm of a young lady who activates the male, makes him creative and regenerative, and keeps everyone moving in life. She is eternally impregnated by the father heaven and yet remains eternally virgin and young. Her fertility, creativity and bounty protect and maintain the masses, the rulers and the state. This belief has led to the establishment of the temples of Kumari, the Living Virgin Goddess, in all three cities of the Kathmandu Valley.

---

[5] This ritual takes place when the girl is close to attaining puberty. She is confined to a dark room and is forbidden from seeing any male and the sunlight. The ceremony is called '*barah tegu*' to symbolize the sign of the Zodiac. The blindfolded girl is then made to look at the Sun, the God of the Sky and her husband. She herself symbolizes the Earth.

Attaining Puberty: Menstruation

Women's sexuality and sexual behaviour are closely scrutinized. Menstruation marks an important milestone in a woman's life. It marks the sexual maturation of her body and transition from a pre-sexual to a sexual being. Among Brahmins and Chhettris, menstrual blood—'the central physiological symbol of female sexuality' (Bennet, 1983)—is a strong source of pollution. Hence, for three days during her period, a woman is not allowed to enter the kitchen, or touch food, water and, in many instances, even fruit trees and vegetables. She is not allowed to touch men and is made to sleep separately from other family members. She is kept in seclusion in a dark room and is not permitted to see the faces of her father, brothers and other men for twelve days. In the mid and far western regions, menstruating women are made to live in a place removed from the home, a practice known as *chhaupadi*. During this time, a woman is treated as an 'untouchable' and is secluded in confinement away from other members of the family, usually in a cowshed, for four days. Such confinement has led to many unfortunate incidents, including deaths. After four days in seclusion, she takes a bath early in the morning and resumes her normal life. From this belief and practice of seclusion and confinement arises 'a vague sense of sin' among women, making them feel lower and ritually less pure than men (Bennet, 1983). Although with the spread of education, the stringency of this practice is waning in urban areas, the notion of impurity and pollution attached to menstruation and menstrual blood remains strong in rural areas. It is perceived as a matter of shame, rather than a normal biological process, by Brahmin and Chhetri women, and they still feel ashamed to talk about such issues. This ritual is less stringent among Tibeto-Burman-speaking ethnic groups who remain more flexible and comfortable during the period and do not go through these rituals.

However, there is one significant connotation associated with menstruation, ie fertility. This symbolizes that the woman is now mature enough to bear children, a characteristic which is highly valued in society. Also, it is believed that menstrual blood is instrumental in the bearing of children. Thus, this ambivalence towards menstrual blood continues. In fact, it provides space to work against seclusion and for empowerment. It is necessary to expose and challenge this ambivalence and duality of perspective concerning menstrual blood. Similarly, a struggle is called for at the level of biological and physiological discourses to relieve women from the burden and spell of associated guilt. In rural areas, people generally associate menstrual blood with a particularly fertile period, and sexual intercourse on the fourth day of menses is considered favourable for conception and appropriate for *ritudan*[6]. During the menstrual period, when women are charged with sexual desire, they are secluded and subjected to cleansing rituals. This is geared to cleanse their sexuality every month and direct it to its 'legitimate end'—the production of children (Bennet, 1983:218).

Social Attitude towards Sexuality and Premarital Sex

In Hindu tradition and culture, contradictory meanings have been attached to the female sex, inspiring both positive and negative feelings. Essentially, a negative view of sex is exhibited, focusing on the 'dangerous' sexual and seductive aspects of a woman. In her study of Shiva mythology, O'Flaherty has demonstrated that asceticism and fertility are closely related themes in the Hindu way of life. Although in human terms, asceticism is opposed to sexuality and fertility, in mythological terms, *tapas* (asceticism) is a power-creating force. The belief is that control and abstinence produce purity and power. Within this framework, spiritual power and sexual power merge. Asceticism, abstinence and discipline form a crucial part of patrilineal ideology. Sexuality is legitimate if it is disciplined by the rules of *gotra* exogamy and caste endogamy (Bennett, 1983:127). At the biological level, total abstinence is incompatible with the continued existence of the patriline. Sexual restraint is central to the overall restraint and control placed on men and women. The sexual restraint of boys and girls in their early years prepares them for the subsequent stage of marriage, as they amass sexual powers for reproductive functions or progeny.

Some form of *Devi* is present in every *kul*[7]. Only when a woman goes to live with her husband does she achieve her full religious and social identities (Bennet, 1983). Both hill and Terai Brahmin communities are generally very conservative in terms of female sexuality and behaviour. Emphasis is placed on restraining and subsuming expressions of desire, particularly those of girls and women. Heterosexuality is the only acceptable norm. The whole arena of sex, sexuality and body is

---

[6] *Ritudan* is the process in which a man gives his seed to a woman which causes her to conceive.

[7] A *kul* is a kinship group which claims a common descent.

surrounded by myths, rules and taboos. People do not mention their genitals by name as it would be embarrassing for the audience to hear. Even between couples these words are not generally used, nor do they utter publicly other words related with sexual acts. The concept of *kanyadan* is very central and presupposes that a woman remains a virgin until she is married. Knowledge of premarital sex and pregnancy is stigmatic and damaging to the marriage prospects of a girl. However, attitudes towards male sexuality and behaviour are more permissive and liberal. Little research has been done in this area and even much less information is available with regard to the attitudes and practices across caste and ethnic groups. Sexual relations are primarily accepted as a means to continue the lineage. The 'high caste' groups, Brahmin and Chhetri, and Newar rarely officially endorse such relations for the sake of pleasure. For an overwhelming majority of women in these groups, the idea of right to body and sexuality is not understandable.

Among some ethnic groups of Nepal, particularly Sherpas, young men and women enjoy the freedom of having sexual relations before marriage. In many cases, in these communities, sexual relations may take place before marriage more or less freely, though they are not openly accepted. In the views of many, sexual relations are permissible so long as no offspring is produced. However, most ethnic groups do not allow prenuptial freedom. They value chastity and virginity. If a girl's sexual relations before marriage are known about, this generally damages her marriage prospects. In marital relations, fidelity is generally considered to be an ideal for both men and women. But this is expected more from women than from men, and there are several ethnic groups which tolerate infidelity.

Among Tamang communities, love affairs among unmarried girls and boys do not damage their future marriage prospects (Bista, 2001). Young Rai and Limbu boys and girls enjoy freedom of movement, and are free to indulge in romance and to make advances to almost any partner, except those prohibited by common descent and close kinship. It is not a big issue for a girl to become pregnant before marriage. In such cases, her lover is expected to accept her as his wife or to pay a certain amount for leaving her. Having a child before marriage is not considered a serious disqualification (ibid). The sexual code of conduct is rather more stringent among different peoples of the Terai, particularly among Brahmins, Rajputs, Bhumihars and Kayasthas. Muslims are also less liberal in sexual matters. The popular traditional practice is to marry at the early age of ten or twelve years (ibid). The Satars of the eastern Terai, however, have traditionally enjoyed absolute freedom in premarital sexual activities. In case of pregnancy before marriage, the lover is expected to marry the mother of his baby or at least find her a husband. The Dolpo people are also very relaxed in sexual matters. There is no prejudice against premarital unions. If an unmarried girl becomes pregnant, her lover must pay the villagers some barley, which is brewed into beer and enjoyed by all (ibid).

From all available accounts, traditionally the 'virtue' of a woman is not only considered to be valuable for the woman herself but to her whole family and kin as well. Cultural tradition has constructed the image, norms and virtues that an ideal woman should possess. These norms, attributes and virtues define certain ways of being a sexually 'normal' Nepali woman and mark other expressions and interpretations as unviable, deviant, abnormal and suspect.

It has not been possible to enter the life worlds, life histories, memories, hopes, values and sufferings of women at the grass roots. However, from the information collected from secondary sources, it appears that, from an early age, a young woman's socialization is geared to make her 'an obedient and dutiful' wife in the home of her future in-laws. She is prepared for modesty, submissiveness and sexually restrained behaviour. Many 'dos' and 'don'ts' in terms of dress, language (including body language), movement, eating manners and manners in relation to parents, husband, in-laws and strangers are to be learnt. She is considered the flag-bearer of the *ijjat* (prestige) and reputation of her parents and family. The more submissive, obedient, courteous and caring she is, the higher the *ijjat* of her parents. Any lapse on the part of the girl with regard to sexual morality is not tolerated and brings disrepute to her father's family. Similar conduct on the part of the boy is more or less ignored. There is a saying that the character of women is as fragile as glass (*sisa jastai najuk*).

Marriage and Conjugal Relations

Weddings take place on specific months and days thought to be auspicious. A young daughter is considered a sacred object who brings *punya* (a reward for a meritorious deed, which opens the door to heaven after death) and fortune to her parents. Traditionally, it was believed that the girl must be married before she attains puberty. *Kanyadan*, when the parents of the bride make a gift of her to the groom, has a deep social and religious significance and, therefore, should take place at the exact moment calculated by the priest (Bista, 2001). This ritual is observed by Newars as well with a slight variation, as illustrated by *Kumari* worship. The goddess ceases to inhabit young girls after menstruation or bleeding or loss of teeth or other forms of serious disease.

For the majority of people, the bond of marriage is the only gateway to sexual experience. Traditionally, marriage is primarily a union for the production of children. Because of this social function, the sexual life of married people is affected not merely by individual desires and varying proficiencies in the art of making love but also by family and societal norms pertaining to sex and expectations as well as concepts of shame and sin. People see marriage as an act of fate and as a manifestation of unseen forces which rule human life. As the subject is taboo, an overwhelming majority of young people enter marriage with no sexual experience, although they develop some kind of awareness indirectly through their own observation or from other sources of family and culture. Conforming to patriarchy and heterosexuality, monogamous marriage within the caste largely has been the only accepted form of union. It is within this institution that the popular imagination of 'sexual bliss' is situated. Sex is a very personal and intimate experience which should be performed in privacy, within closed premises and away from the public gaze. Forms of open bodily and sexual expressions and intimations in public places are not appreciated and are considered vulgar and refractory. Even among men, though vulgarity is tolerated to a greater extent, disruptive refractions are disliked and certain behaviours are penalized. One instance is the practice of *jari*, ie the compensation paid by a man to the husband of the woman he takes away. Generally, among the middle class, restrained sexuality is respected because it operates within socially sanctioned norms, and is instrumental in the maintenance and reproduction of the system.

Though quantitative data are not consistent, the mean age of marriage is 15 and 18 years in the Terai and in the hill and mountain districts respectively. A WHO survey (2000) reports that 3.2 per cent of respondents are married by the age of 15 years and 36 per cent by 18 years. Child marriage is prohibited by law, but in many cases customary practices are still honoured and punishment for violators too light to serve as a deterrent, even if the laws are properly enforced. As communities and the larger society still largely accept this custom, people refrain from reporting cases to the police, who do not take action unless a formal complaint is lodged (Dhital, 2007). The consequences of early marriage are many. It is associated with health risks, pregnancies, complications during delivery, including death, underdeveloped poorly brought up babies, early school dropouts and so on. However, the practice still persists as a means to control female behaviour and sexuality.

There are many barriers that come in the way of an individual's free will in the choosing of a marriage partner. Any one factor such as class, caste, ethnic group, social norms and religion can obstruct this choice. All these institutions constantly police the activities of individuals. Of late, there has been a laxity in these matters. Intercaste marriages are increasingly common, and in some cases such marriages are carried out with the consent of both families. However, intercaste marriage, particularly between high caste Hindus and Dalits is rare and still looked down upon in spite of the legal ban on caste-based discrimination.

Although marriage and sexual relations are largely monogamous, incidents of polygamy are found quite often among certain groups. Caste endogamy is a norm, but sometimes in the case of men, marrying a girl of a 'lower' caste is acceptable. Arranged marriage is the rule and in many cases parents do not deem it necessary to seek the consent of the girl. In Newar communities, the girl is married to the *Bel* fruit before she attains puberty. Her subsequent marriage is considered to be of secondary importance and, therefore, cannot nullify this marriage. Incidents of love marriage have been increasing in recent times, especially among economically better-off educated urban groups. Other forms of marriage include cross-cousin marriage (among Thakuris, Gurungs, Magars), marriage by capture (among Tamangs, Thakalis, Rai-Limbus, Sunuwars and Jirels) and so on. The practice of elopement can be found more or less in all communities, more frequently among ethnic communities. Fraternal polyandry is practised among Sherpa communities, where brothers may jointly marry one or more common wives. But more than two brothers cannot marry jointly. Polyandry, whereby a wife can have several husbands, is also practised by the Manangba in the western high mountains and the people of Kimathanka in the north eastern mountains. The reasons attributed to this practice are poverty and a desire to avoid partition of property. The wife of the eldest brother has to serve as the wife of a younger brother as well, even though the law does not recognize it. However, the wife of a younger brother cannot serve as the wife of an elder brother (Majpuria, 1982). A wife can demand compensation from an adulterous woman having sexual relations with her husband. Similarly, an offended husband can claim compensation from a man having illicit sexual relations with his wife.

Thus, marriage customs vary from one ethnic group to another, and different rules are practised in different communities. However, certain rules are more generally applied. Among different ethnic groups in the hills and mountains, a marriage bond is not absolutely binding and divorce also is more informal. Some instances of elopement do occur among Brahmins, Chhetris and Newars, but elopement is not appreciated and is more commonly found among ethnic groups. In some cases marriage between cousins is permitted, whereas in some other groups it is strictly prohibited. Among Muslims, marriage is permitted between a half-brother and a half-sister where they are children of one father by different mothers or one mother from different fathers. Child marriage is common in Tharu communities. However, in such cases, there is generally a long interval between engagement and marriage.

In many joint families, relations between husband and wife are restricted by curtailing the free time they can spend together. Similarly, the woman's relationship with the elder brother of her husband is highly restricted. Respect and avoidance between husband and wife minimize the conflict between the role of a son and that of a husband for a young married man and also serves to eliminate any suspicion of sexual relations between the daughter-in-law and other male in-laws. While following the strictly prescribed mutual behaviour patterns, it is of the wife's *dharma* to be obedient, respectful, faithful and pleasing to the husband. Sex as a means to have children and to influence their husbands in their favour is their most effective weapon in the battle for security and respect in the husband's house (Bennett, 1983:176-7). Although inhibitions are demonstrated while talking seriously about their physical and emotional responses, sexual and suggestive jokes and exchanges abound among women. However, they feel it improper to admit sexual pleasure. Similarly, overt expressions of attraction by a husband towards his wife are not appreciated; so, romantic affection and sexuality are expressed covertly in private spaces.

Therefore, daughters-in-law try to present themselves as ideals of modesty, shyness, obedience and submissiveness and, in the house of their in-laws, move around with downcast eyes, covering most of their body. Constant guarding and surveillance are considered necessary as the patriline's purity of descent is made vulnerable by the affinal women who must bear its next generation. It is obvious that if a woman's sexuality is not guarded, the offspring of other men from other lineages and even other castes may be mistakenly incorporated (Bennett, 1983:125). Her only influence in the joint family is through her husband. To gain power, she must use her sexuality to win him away from his ingrained loyalties to his parents and brothers (Bennet, 1983:219). There is a belief that the wife's integrity, chastity and faithfulness increase the lifespan of her husband. Legends have it that the power of *sati*—a woman who is completely faithful to her husband—can even defer or alter divine interventions.

In fact, there is a pronounced ambivalence that governs the wife–husband relationship. As Kakar (2007:18) notes, the age-old cultural splitting of a wife into a mother and a whore, a well known Freudian syndrome, is also exhibited in the Hindu view of women. The men are thus torn between the objects of desire and adoration. Man idealizes one kind of woman as 'higher' and 'purer' than him, with whom he cannot have sexual relations, while, on the other hand, he is capable of sexual relations with women of lower social status such as prostitutes. The splitting of a woman's image into a goddess and a whore allows man to have a modicum of sexual life without being overwhelmed by anxiety (ibid). So, from the perspective of psychoanalysis, it is essential for a man to see his wife in the image of a whore in order to be sexually potent. The image of a whore is inherently promiscuous, full of passion, harbouring illicit desires and capable of being heartless and unfaithful at the first opportunity. Therefore, she needs to be kept under strict discipline and surveillance within and outside the family. There are strong rules (though arguably becoming weaker) which are concerned with the regulation of sex and food, both areas where desire for the flesh is strong, for the maintenance of ritual purity. In many instances, even the dress and behavioural codes are prescribed for young women and mothers.

A couple is expected to maintain a balance between asceticism and fertility (Bennet, 1983:44). Sexual love is considered the keenest pleasure known to the senses, but is also felt to be destructive to a man's physical and spiritual well-being. Women are powerful, demanding, seductive and ultimately destructive. During the Teej festival, the high spirits, the flirtatiousness, the sexuality which 'high caste' women must ordinarily suppress are released en masse at Shiva's temples. However, this display of the erotic side of the female nature is only permissible because, on Teej, it is held in check by the strict purifying fast which the women are undergoing for the welfare of their husbands (ibid).

Motherhood

The transition to motherhood gradually begins to transform the daughter-in-law's situation and status in the family. In Hindu, Buddhist and *Tantric* traditions, the mother is a revered figure with high ritual status and a source of all power and energy. She symbolizes female purity and is an idealized figure men fear. In the Nepali context, the concept of the divine feminine fuses with 'mother'. While the wife is associated with pollution, menstrual blood, potential unfaithfulness and sexual demands, the mother is a creator, nourisher and a repository of selfless and asexual love. All goddesses are called 'mother': Laxmi Mata, Saraswoti Mata, Durga Mata, Kali Mata, Devi Mata and so on. Mothers are respected as goddesses, as a mother is also seen as a creator and protector. A band of goddesses are labelled *Matrikas*—'mothers'. The earth is *'Dharati Mata'* (Mother Earth), and is worshipped in reverence for Her stability and the inexhaustible fecundity possessed by Her. She is also a creator and nourisher. She is understood as a great living being and cosmic microcosm possessing anthropomorphic characteristics (Kinsley 1998:178). Rivers are also perceived as mothers and worshipped. The land of the country is also considered mother—'Nepal Amaa'.

As Bennet notes, female sexuality is not denied in the mother, but it is transformed and legitimized by its manifest service to the patriline. According to Bennet, motherhood purifies the affinal women from dangerous wives of one generation and transforms them into the consanguineal women of the next. Her threatening and highly sexual identity as a wife is increasingly overlaid by her role as a mother (Bennet: 256). After delivery, women are more confident and less strict in their dress codes and behaviour. Newly delivered women are allowed to sun-bathe with their legs and breasts exposed.

Thus, a woman is revered as a goddess when she is a virgin and later highly respected as a mother. So, the time between the two states in which women are most sexually active is considered to be dangerous. Accordingly, they are placed under stringent codes, which regulate their behaviour.

Divorce and Widowhood

Divorce confers freedom on women from oppressive conjugal bonds, atrocities, torture and harassment. Traditionally, divorce was not practised by the 'high caste' Brahmins and Chhetris and other Hindu caste groups. Among Newars it used to be easier as the wife could become free by returning the areca nuts she had received from her husband during their wedding (Bista, 2001). However, high caste Newars rarely practise this provision. Divorce was easier among different indigenous communities where women could leave their husbands and take another husband if the latter husband compensated the former. Among people in Dolpo divorce can be achieved by either the husband or the wife paying a certain amount of money to the other partner (ibid: 197). Danuwar, Majhi and Darai women can leave their husbands, but the new husband has to compensate the former one. No comprehensive facts and figures are available on the incidence, trends and reasons for divorce for the country as a whole. One recent study of divorce in Pokhara Valley has shown increasing incidence of divorce among the traditionally more conservative high caste Hindu women. Between 2030 and 2055, out of a total of 326 cases of divorce registered in Kaski District Court, 173 were from Brahmin and 153 from Chhetri families. The two most important reasons for divorce were found to be an unbalanced sexual life and physical and mental torture and oppression within the family (Baral, 2003). This figure should be taken with caution. As members of more remote ethnic groups do not need to take recourse to the court, their divorces may go unregistered. Accordingly, the real figure of divorces may be higher than recorded.

Hindu traditions do not allow a widow to remarry. Taboos about marriage of a widow and the need for her to practise abstinence from luxuries are strictly observed among high caste Hindus. The restrictions imposed on remarriage by religious and social norms offset the actual materialization of the privilege of remarriage guaranteed by the Naya Muluki Ain. Consequently, post-widowhood celibacy is still being practised by a large proportion of the population.

A widow's sexuality is similar to that of an unmarried pubescent girl—a social anomaly. Since she is no longer under the control of her husband, she presents a potential problem to both her affinal and consanguineal kins. Of late, though the law has become permissive regarding widow remarriage, the social practice has yet to gain momentum. Among the Sherpa, Manangba and Baragaule, the widow of an elder brother will automatically become the wife of his younger brother, but a man has no right over the widow of his brother. There is no stigma attached to a young man marrying an elderly widow or a divorcee among Tamang communities as well. Rai and Limbu men can also marry an elder brother's widow or a deceased wife's sister. Some other groups like Danuwar, Majhi and Darai allow the marriage of elder brother's widow but not the younger brother's widow. The Satars of the eastern Terai also practise marriage with the elder brothers' widow. Among Muslims, there is no stigma attached to widow remarriage.

Sexual Minorities

Traditionally, these groups have remained invisible in Nepali society. No stories or accounts are available to depict their lives and world. As heterosexuality has been long constructed as the 'norm', knowledge of a person's involvement in an 'unnatural' sexual act would not only turn her/him instantly into an outcast, but also subject her/him to stigma, sanctions and harassment from the common people as well as from government authorities. Until very recent times, there was no Lesbian, Gay, Bisexual and Transgender (LGBT) identity or activism. Unlike in India, where the third gender, ie *hijaras*, have a long tradition, Nepali society till very recently was largely oblivious to their existence and insensitive to their rights and needs. As heterosexuality was the norm, 'other' sexualities were marginalized and repressed. Similarly, the sexuality of people with disabilities has largely been ignored. Of late, with the advent of multiparty democracy, liberal ideas and rights-based discourses, these minorities have gained some visibility to the extent that an activist has been elected to Nepal's Constituent Assembly. The Blue Diamond Society, Mitini and similar organizations are championing the cause of sexual minorities. These initiatives have helped to bring underground lesbian and gay cultures gradually to the surface and have encouraged many to engage in LGBT politics.

Changing Perceptions and Practices

The proliferation of sexuality and human rights-based discourses, as well as a revolution in the print and audio-visual media, has in some ways expanded both the spaces where women and men can be sexual and the ways in which they might be sexual. The advent of the HIV/AIDS pandemic has called for more compelling debates on the issues of sexuality and bodily integrity. The emergence of sexual minority activism as well as discourses promoting social inclusion have opened new vistas for engagement.

With the explosive advent of technological revolutions and their global imports, the influences on human bodies have multiplied. Wombs are made and sold, genetic engineering is carried out in foreign laboratories, sex and sexuality can be assigned. Abortion (and hymenorrhaphy in the Muslim world) is becoming more common. Similarly, music videos have fired the sexual imagination and inspired new fantasies. Teleserials and movies with explicit and implicit sexual content are normalizing new ways of looking at sexuality and the human body. Voices and solidarities of different marginalized and repressed groups and expressions are getting louder. Conventional stereotypes are slowly being melted down and challenged. Struggles for identity, representation, inclusion and non-discrimination by hitherto marginalized groups, including sexual minorities, are now becoming much more visible. No doubt, for a large number of people, these emerging issues remain taboos, for some they are 'dirty' and for others they are trivial when compared to more significant problems and issues confronting the country such as poverty, a war-torn economy, disease, illiteracy and socio-economic transformation.

Writing in the Indian context, Lata Mani (2009:195-7) has explored the relationship between today's neo-liberal free market economy and the new spaces it creates, where the 'body' (or more specifically one's sexuality) can be viewed, admired, enhanced, rejuvenated and beautified. Nepali citizens, too, are consumers of these 'spaces', which have been created by new modes of media consumption and the increased reach of advertising; dozens of billboards above New Road, newly built boutiques along Durbar Marg, and the plethora of beauty, fashion and health-related magazines now available in any city in Nepal attest to the fact that many Nepali have become integrated into what one writer has described as the 'global family' (Shakya, 2009:55).

Mani writes further how perceiving the 'body' in South Asia has changed significantly with recent advances in technology and increases in media and advertising consumption (2009:195-7). In our 'neo-liberal present', she writes '... the body is not merely subject to desire. It is also the object of desire. Indeed the body is desire incarnate. In consuming that which it desires, the body is able to enhance its own desirability. Such desirability is most often coded in sexual terms. This is so because qualities such as power, aesthetics, strength and success are increasingly articulated around the axis of sexuality. It is thus that sexually explicit advertising has become ubiquitous. Wherever we turn, we are beckoned by pouting lips, smouldering eyes and virtually naked male and female bodies. In a way, not to be seen even in the West that we are supposed to be emulating, our public spaces are festooned by advertising that is frequently nothing other than soft porn.'

It is in this new context that Nepali women are not only expected to be virtuous but also sexually attractive. Beauty, clothing and body shapes are cherished. So, what are the new and liberating aspects of new expressions of sexuality? These are areas for further investigation and research. Heterosexual marriage is one of our most conventional, normative and patriarchal institutions. It is within this institution that popular images of domestic sexual bliss are located. However, these sites are slowly being invaded by new identities, discourses and praxis.

Thus, perceptions, attitudes and behaviours with regard to sexuality are changing rapidly with the times, and diversity is gradually being celebrated. There is diversity even within the ranks of feminist activism, with some groups asking for censorship against the exploitative varieties of the representation of women's bodies, attacking 'obscenity' and the promiscuous nature of 'western culture as a threat to traditional values', while others, demanding space for greater sexual expression, are challenging demands for censorship itself and the policing of sexuality-related space. Particular instances of such debate are beauty pageants. There have been arguments and advocacy for and against them. Voices are also being heard for and against the decriminalization of sex work or prostitution and concerning the issues surrounding dance bars and massage parlours.

State and Sexuality

The state's approach to, and understanding of, sexuality has tended to focus on empowerment, population management and reproductive health rather than on the recognition of citizens as sexual and emotional beings. Policies are basically guided by gender equity and equality perspectives and focus on the elimination of discrimination against women, while protecting and promoting their socio-economic and political rights, gender mainstreaming and targeted programmes for women empowerment, implementation of national and international commitments, women's participation and representation in different state structures, provision and expansion of socio-economic services so as to ensure greater access and the elimination of conditions and practices that are disgraceful and dehumanizing.

Efforts are underway to achieve this through the enactment and reform of policies, plans, laws and structures, such as the introduction of national action plans, the establishment of the Women's Commission, the creation of the posts of Women Development Officers and Gender Focal Points and amendments in legal provisions, the engendering of the development process (through mainstreaming, targeted programmes, gender budgets and gender audits), provision and expansion of socio-economic services (in education, health, drinking water, awareness, empowerment initiatives) and affirmative actions (quotas in the civil service, local government bodies and the recent resolution in parliament for 33 per cent representation of women). Similarly, emphasis is given to the promotion of physical and mental health and reducing the incidence and effects of gender-based violence, and also expanding reproductive and sexual health services. Government has also expanded reproductive health services for the youth down to community level, tried to improve maternal health, expanded HIV/AIDS and STD Control and anti-retroviral treatment (ART) programmes, streamlined family planning and safe motherhood programmes, and attempted to tackle all forms of violence against women and trafficking in women and children. However, while the Three-Year Interim Plan (TYIP) lays emphasis on ensuring the sexual and reproductive health rights of women, it does not spell out how this is to be achieved. In brief, the government's perspective equates women's empowerment with improvements in their social, economic and political power and participation, along with the expansion of access to social and economic services. All policy, legal and institutional reforms are, therefore, geared to that end.

Recent Positive Steps in Legislation

Traditionally, marriage laws in Nepal are said to have been deeply influenced by Brahmanical concepts. One such concept demands a higher standard of sexual restraint from women than from men and accordingly, a woman may marry and have legitimate sexual relations with a single man—her husband. The only honourable form of marriage is *Kanyadan*. Purity in women is also essential to maintain purity of descent and caste hierarchy. The higher the group in the caste hierarchy, the greater the concern is for ritual purity and control of female sexuality.

The TYIP emphasizes social inclusion for excluded and marginalized groups. For the first time in Nepali history, a formally recognized representative of a sexual minority has been elected as a member of the Constituent Assembly and the budget of FY2065/66 has initiated a new programme for the support of sexual and gender minorities. In the last few years, the government has shown more tolerance towards lesbian and gay activists and organizations. Legal reforms have been initiated to criminalize marital rape and decriminalize abortion and sexual orientations and expressions previously deemed 'abnormal'. An abortion law came into effect in 2002, which allows a woman to terminate her pregnancy under the following conditions: pregnancies of twelve weeks or less for any woman; pregnancies of eighteen weeks' gestation if the pregnancy is the result of rape or incest; pregnancies of any duration with the recommendation of an authorized medical practitioner if the life of the mother is at risk on account of her physical or mental health or the foetus is deformed. The law prohibits abortion without the consent of the pregnant woman, sex selective abortions and abortions performed outside the legally permissible criteria. However, the level of awareness among women about this legal provision is very low; the Nepal Demographic and Health Survey (NDHS) shows that only one in three women is aware that abortion is legal in Nepal. Thirteen per cent of women respondents in the 15-49 age group, mostly from the 35-39 age group, reported an abortion or miscarriage in the five years preceding survey (2007:152-3).

A landmark verdict recently given by the Supreme Court directs the government to reform discriminatory policies and legal provisions. So far, these reforms and changes have been of a more symbolic nature, indicating that attitudes of the state towards sexual minorities and the issues of sexuality, sexual rights, sexual orientation or preference, bodily integrity, personhood and sexuality education remain largely to be addressed. There is also no consensus on whether the state is consciously repressive towards female sexuality and still a great deal of confusion regarding sexual minoritie. Activists also remain unclear as to whether, and to what extent, the state should, or should not, exert direct or indirect control over the sexuality and bodies of its citizens, or what would be the measure of 'reasonable regulation'. The good news is that the debate has begun.

Field Work

To gain impressions from the grass roots, fieldwork was carried out in three VDCs of Baglung district, namely Lekhani, Bhimpokhara and Bhiun. Based on interviews with key informants and focus group discussions, some information was generated to gauge the local attitudes and estimate the level of awareness of sexuality and sex-related issues.

During the field work it was found that people generally found words such as *younikta* and *laingikta* incomprehensible. Informants explained they felt uncomfortable talking about sexuality, as sexuality was invariably equated with sex. Women and men felt awkward even asking for contraceptives in shops. However, after the ice was broken, they gradually began to participate in the discussions. Generally, women participants did not share issues related with their sex and sexuality with their husbands. Women are unable to express their resentment even during pregnancy, menstruation, etc. Men generally do not appreciate women's needs and problems. Very few women shared their problems with their friends, daughters and mothers-in-law. Neither did husbands generally discuss these issues with their wives. Even young people did not have appropriate and adequate information to enable them to make informed decisions. Those who had been previously trained in reproductive health issues, such as female community health volunteers (FCHVs), found it easier to understand and discuss the issues openly.

Impressions from Surveys and Fieldwork

Sexual initiation, contraception and attitudes towards premarital sex

A survey of school and college students of Kathmandu and Kaski Districts found the mean age of first sex to be 16.3 years. Eighty-eight per cent of the students had seen condoms and 91 per cent of sexually initiated youth had used them. Out of the sexuality initiated groups, 24 per cent reported they had had sex against their will. Most of the students (86.4%) were in favour of sex education in school. Altogether 27.4 per cent of students thought it okay to have premarital sex. For 44 per cent, friends were the most important source of information and knowledge about sex. Of the respondents, 25.6 per cent were currently in love affairs, out of which 14.7 per cent reported sexual relations (Gautam, 2004).

According to the Nepal Demographic and Health Survey (2006), only 8 per cent of young women and 4 per cent of young men had had sex by age 15, while 47 per cent of young women and 27 per cent of young men had had sex by age 18. The male/female difference in the age of sexual debut is primarily due to an earlier marriage age among women. A lower percentage of women and men in the 18-19 age group had initiated sex before age 18 than those in the 20-24 age group. Less than 1 per cent of women with SLC and higher education had their first sexual encounter before the age of 15 and about 11 per cent had initiated sexual intercourse before 18. Only 5 per cent of young women and 26 per cent of young men used condoms in their first sexual encounters. Unmarried male youth were more likely to have used a condom. About 83 per cent of never married young men had never had sexual intercourse. Premarital sexual intercourse among young men is more frequent at older ages, in urban areas, in the mountains and hill areas, among the highly educated and wealthiest quintiles and among those who has travelled away from home for more than six months. Almost all never married women reported not having had sex.

A Knowledge, Attitude, Practice and Skills Survey was carried out by MSI (2001) among Nepalese teenagers in the age group of 12-18. A total of 1,400 teenagers were randomly selected from across the country. An equal number of girls and boys were selected (723 from urban centres and 677 from rural areas). The study shows that almost 20 per cent of teenagers consider premarital sex as proper. One in five boys and nearly one in ten girls interviewed had had sexual experience. Sixty-five per cent of boys said that they had used condoms, while 74 per cent of girls said that their partners used a condom during sexual intercourse. Unprotected sex led to a 14 per cent pregnancy rate and 22 per cent of STD infection rate among boys and 13 per cent among girls.

The findings also showed that Nepali teenagers were highly aware of HIV risks, but this awareness does not guarantee safe sex behaviour.

Although an overwhelming majority (92%) of teenagers had heard of HIV/AIDS, only 74 per cent knew that condoms should be used while having sex. One in five boys and nearly one in ten girls interviewed had had sexual experience. Sixty-five per cent of boys said that they had used condoms, while 74 per cent of girls said that their partners used the condom during sexual intercourse. Unprotected sex led to a 22 per cent STD infection rate in boys and a 13 per cent rate in girls as well as a 14 per cent pregnancy rate.

Most teenagers said they were interested in learning more about sex and sexual health. They wanted more information about STDs/HIV/AIDS and safe sex. Radio and television were the best sources of information on HIV/AIDS. Clubs were also good places to learn about sex and HIV/AIDS. These are all sources of learning without parental knowledge (MSI, 2001).

Sexual violence

Attitudes towards wife-beating have also undergone changes over the years. The NDHS survey sought opinion on beating based on five optional reasons, ie in case she burns the food, argues with him, goes out without telling him, neglects the children, and refuses to have sexual intercourse with him. Twenty-three per cent of women believed that beating was justified for at least one of the five reasons, as compared to 29 per cent in 2001. The most widely accepted reason (20%) among women was the neglecting of children. Only 3 per cent of women believed that a man was justified in beating his wife for refusing him sex. The proportion of men who gave this as a reason for beating was also 3 per cent. This also indicates an improvement in the attitude of men towards wife-beating over the last five years. Women with no education and from the lower wealth quintile were more likely to justify beating (2007:233).

Sexual empowerment has important implications for demographic and health outcomes such as the transmission of HIV/AIDS and other STDs. It is also an indicator of women's overall empowerment because it measures a woman's level of acceptance of the norm in certain societies which believes that women do not have the agency or right to refuse intercourse with their husbands or possess full control over their body and sexuality. It also reflects sexual roles and women's sense of self-esteem. The recent NDHS also tried to capture attitudes and behaviour in this regard. The respondents were given three options for refusing sexual advances from their husbands: in cases she knows her husband has an STD; knows husband has had sexual intercourse with another woman; and she is tired or not in mood. Overall, the majority of men and women agreed that each of the specified options could be a justified reason for refusing sexual intercourse with her husband (83% of women and 79% of men). The most accepted reason for refusing was the knowledge of the STD status of the husband (2007:236).

Information, education and sexuality

Movies, magazines and books provide information and stimulation regarding sex and sexuality. However, no systematic efforts are in the offing to educate children and adolescents about sexual matters. In this context, the issue of sex education is important. In Nepali culture, parents cannot handle this matter effectively as they harbour many inhibitions about discussing sex with their children. In such a situation, the traditional role parents play as role models for young children does not work. The main source of information on sex tends to be friends, audio-visual and print media, as well as school teachers.

However, the information provided by these channels is far from sufficient in providing sex education. Of late, increasing access to the internet has added one more dimension. As society curtails information, the youth resort to illicit sources of information through cyber cafes and pornography. There are increasing reports of school children indulging in such activities.

Sex workers and prostitution

'Sex work' is not recognized as a form of labour or profession in Nepal and remains a huge and unexplored underside of Nepali society. Like the world over, historically, people have engaged in various forms of 'illicit' sexual liaison outside marriage. As the state and society in Nepal have been conservative and repressive towards overt sexual transactions, prostitution has survived and flourished silently at the margins, brought to light only during occasional crackdowns. Girls and women, poverty-stricken or abandoned by husbands and families or trafficked by some luring them with the promises of work are forced to take on sex work as a means of livelihood. One grotesque fact is that vulnerable Nepali girls and women are trafficked in huge numbers (estimates are around ten to twelve thousand a year) to India and abroad to engage in forced sexual labour. Of late, with the liberalization of the economy in Nepal, new forms of entertainment business have flourished, which have provided opportunities for sex work for quite a number of women and men. Dance restaurants and bars and massage parlours in different parts of the country are some examples of these. Sex work is one of the most vulnerable professions in Nepal and grossly ignored and unprotected by the state. As sex work is criminalized, sex workers are regularly subjected to harassment and blackmail by police and others. There are voices being raised from certain quarters for decriminalization of sex work.

Sexuality and HIV/AIDS

Thanks to the efforts made by government and non-government sectors, people are gradually becoming aware of the risks of HIV/AIDS. According to NDHS, 28 per cent of women and 44 per cent of men in the 15-24 age group have comprehensive knowledge about HIV/AIDS. This knowledge is higher among the youth who have never been married. Forty-three per cent of urban young women and 25 per cent of rural young women have comprehensive knowledge. Higher proportions of women from the hills, the central hill sub region, with SLC and higher education, and from higher wealth quintiles have comprehensive knowledge. Seventy-three per cent of women and 92 per cent of men in the 15-49 age groups had heard of AIDS. Similarly, 69 per cent of rural women and 91 per cent of urban women had heard of it. Hill women are more aware than women in the mountains and Terai. Awareness is strongly related to education and wealth.

According to NDHS, HIV/AIDS prevention programmes focus on three areas of behaviour: delayed sexual debut, limiting the number of partners (remaining faithful to one partner) and the use of condoms. Women are most aware (65%) that the chances of getting infected can be reduced by limiting sex to one uninfected partner or by abstaining from sexual intercourse (60%). Among men, the most commonly known preventive method was the use of condoms (84%). Younger women and men in the 15-24 age group know more about various methods of prevention than older age groups, with 65 per cent of women and 83 per cent of men in the 15-24 age group reporting knowledge of contraception and prevention methods. Knowledge was lowest among those divorced, separated or widowed (2007:202). Education has a positive impact on awareness.

Attitudes towards negotiating safe sex

Generally, women are thought to be passive recipients of male initiative, and are not supposed to possess the agency to refuse or negotiate sex. However, things seem to be changing in recent times. According to NDHS, 94 per cent of women and 95 per cent of men believe that a woman is justified in refusing sex if she knows that her husband is

Badis

Mainly living in ten districts in the Mid and Far West Nepal, Badis are one of the most disadvantaged communities in Nepal. It is believed that this community originated sometime in the fourteenth century. Thakuri kings of western Nepal used to keep *Rajnartakis* (female royal dancers) for entertainment and gradually over subsequent generations these dancers became concubines, forming a community over time. Living as a nomadic community, dancing and singing, they used to move from place to place, being paid for their performances. In the beginning, apart from a few illegal relationships with feudal lords they did not practise prostitution. They used to earn their livelihood by dancing and singing on social occasions such as festivals, ceremonies and public foyers. With the advent of modern means of entertainment, the Badis were displaced from their traditional occupation and were left without any alternative means of income. This forced them to adopt prostitution as a means to livelihood, which gradually became their occupation. Partly due to their geographical isolation and partly due to their nomadic tradition, their access to education and skill development opportunities was extremely limited. The women of Badi community took on prostitution as a profession with permission from their husbands and families. The majority of Badis are not able to get married. Of late, government and non-government sectors have been trying to eliminate this practice through various capacity-building, empowerment, income generation and livelihood support interventions. However, the practice still persists in different parts of Mid and Far Western Nepal.

(Adapted with paraphrasing from *South Asia Partnership*, 2001)

infected. Differences by background characteristics are minimal and replies varied only slightly according to the background and caste of respondents. Less than 1 per cent of women reported having multiple sexual partners. Three per cent of men in the 15-49 age group reported having more than two partners during the twelve months preceding the survey. About 6 per cent of men in the same age group reported having high risk intercourse during the past 12 months (2007:211). Less than 1 per cent of men reported that they had engaged in paid sex in the year before the survey. The number of people engaged in, or paying for, sex is slightly higher among migrant Nepalis. Where migration is common, as in the case of Nepal, knowing one's HIV status is especially important for curbing the spread of the infection. It is also important to empower women to negotiate preventive and curative measures to protect themselves and their children.

Thirty-five per cent of women in the 15-49 age group knew where to go for HIV testing (ibid: 213). Four in five women with SLC or higher education knew about the location of such testing facilities. Less than 1 per cent of women and a negligible percentage of men in the 15-49 age group reported having an STD in the last 12 months. But it is likely that these figures underestimate the actual prevalence (ibid: 215).

Recent sexual activities among never married youth

NDHS shows that about 83 per cent of never married young men had never had sexual intercourse. Premarital sexual intercourse among young men is higher in older ages, in urban areas, in the mountain and

Jhuma

The practice of *Jhuma* is observed among Sherpas, a Tibeto-Burman ethnic group living in the northern high mountains of the country. A baby girl is offered as a gift to god and then becomes known as a *Jhuma*. Her role is to perform religious functions and engage in daily work for the monastery throughout her life. She is not allowed to marry but it appears that men seek sexual relations with *Jhumas*. Once again, physical and cultural bondage are the lot of girls and women in caste and ethnic groups with entrenched traditional values.

(Adapted from SAP, 2001)

Deuki/Devaki

Traditional religious and cultural practices of all castes have been found to use girls in different rituals which often undermine their development and life prospects. *Deuki* is one such institution. As in the case of *Devadasis* in India, families of the 'high caste' Chhetris in Far Western Nepal, particularly in Baitadi, pledge daughters or other young girls to deities in temples, seeking special favours from the goddess. They promise the goddess of the temple that, in order to have their prayers answered, they will give their daughters to the temple as offerings. With time, the practice was changed, whereby young girls were bought from poor villagers and left in temples as offerings and gradually people began to buy and give girls to temples for increasingly material reasons: winning elections, buying land, etc. The young girls cannot marry because there is a superstition that misfortune will fall on whoever marry them. Once they are offered to the temple, they are left on their own, forcing them into servitude. *Deukis* and *Devis* end up as mistresses, 'kept wives' or prostitutes. They have children from sexual encounters, and their daughters are called *Devis,* who again are sold by their mothers as offerings. The mother is so poor, and so, if someone wants to buy the daughter to give to the temple, she sells her. The Children's Act forbids the practice and imposes a penalty of five years' imprisonment for offenders, but enforcement has been weak and it was reported that there were around 17,000 girls pledged as *Devakis* in 1992.

(Adapted with paraphrasing from *Children in South Asia* [1998] and Hayward's *Breaking the Earthenware Jar* [2000])

hill areas, among the most highly educated and wealthiest quintiles and among those who have travelled away from home for more than six months. Almost all never married women reported never having had sex (2007:222).

There are other arenas which have not been explored or documented properly such as the practice of black magic and spells to win the love of a man or a woman. It is possible that, as observed by Kakar in India, sexuality is used 'to redress the lopsided distribution of power between the sexes' (2007:14). It is possible that, in Nepal also, sexuality is being deployed as a resource to navigate through or negotiate space in the family or public sphere. Though beyond the scope of this study, it would be interesting to see how far sexuality can be deployed or is actually being deployed as a resource to balance gender relations. On the other hand, ungratifying sexual relations can bring about spells of tension and unhappiness in conjugal and family lives. This is also one area that can be explored further.

4 | FINDINGS

While sex and sexuality are often perceived as personal or private subjects, they have wide-ranging political implications and, once certain categories of sexuality or sexual behaviour are rendered abnormal, there is a hidden assumption that these categories should be restricted, closely guarded and policed. Accordingly, there emerge spaces, norms, boundaries and mechanisms that constantly guard, regulate and ensure the prevalence of the 'normal'. This 'normal' is consistently reinforced by tradition, culture, media, the state, market and economy, as well as by individual practices and progressive internalization.

From the surveys and field work carried out as part of this study, as well as background readings and examinations of various case studies, we can draw these tentative conclusions regarding sexuality in the Nepali context, and how it is viewed among different sections of society. Taking this data into account, and backed by a review of secondary and other literature, our recommendations will be presented in Chapter V.

▸ Sex and sexuality are taboos in Nepali society. People in general and women in particular are hesitant and feel embarrassed to discuss the topic. Many do not even want to talk about it. This hesitation is prevalent in more or less all social classes, castes and ethnic groups in rural areas. Younger and more educated boys and girls, though more forthcoming, are not completely free of this feeling and attitude. People find it not only an uncomfortable topic to deliberate or discuss, but also their understanding of the issue is dismally meagre. Even basic words that are in use in Nepali such as *'laingikta'* and *'younikta'*, are not familiar to rural women. People are not conceptually equipped to engage in fruitful discussion of the issue of sexuality.

▸ The negative view of sex as an unruly, dirty and dangerous drive which needs to be tamed by exercising restraint and disciplinary techniques is so pervasive that anyone openly advocating sexual rights may be looked down upon as a pervert promoting corrupt western sexual mores. Talking about sexuality is also considered to be disruptive to the social order and moral fabric of a 'good' society. The major bloc of society still lags far behind the state and the few progressive pieces of legislation which have recently emerged from it and localities remain the strongholds of patriarchal values and norms.

- Nepali women are not a monolithic or homogenous category. There are multitudes of experiences based on social, religious, economic and regional locations, and it is vital to distinguish which type of woman we are talking about. There are many urban women and elite women belonging to the upper classes who are often educated, independent and economically self-sufficient. It is from this stratum that the leaders of the movement for sexual empowerment have emerged. There, however, remains a huge gulf between this group of women and the home-based workers subjected to different forms of exploitation, harassment and abuse and those who have never seen the world beyond the confines of their home. Though they may join and support the larger and often abstract mainstream agenda led by the elite women, the needs of the subalterns are different and of a more urgent nature. Similarly, the external influences, which control much of a woman's body, sexuality and choice, are often not uniform, thus requiring different sets of strategies.

- Glaring contradictions and inconsistencies are noted in the way people view the divine image of the feminine and the feminine of the 'real world'. It is intriguing that those who devote themselves to the worship of the divine feminine assign women such a low place within the household and society, ignoring their own suggestions that women are *Devis*—the female principles in our lives. Laxmi, Saraswoti and various forms of Shakti and her extensions are worshipped. But in real life the same principles are discarded. In short, the divine feminine is worshipped, while the human feminine is oppressed. What is revered in the divine is not tolerated in human beings. While the *Raas Leela* of Krishna and his *Gopis* are hailed, the extramarital affair of Radha endorsed, in real life such freedom is not permitted. Another instance is erotic carving in temples. People never question such artefacts and yet hesitate or find it embarrassing even to talk and discuss erotica. These contradictions and dualisms sometimes reach the level of open hypocrisy.

▶ Sex and sexuality are culturally and religiously regulated, and accepted types of sexual behaviour are learnt through socialization. Despite the differences in behaviour between different caste and ethnic groups, this is an important general aspect of individual and social life. For all caste and ethnic groups, sex fulfils varying social functions relating to procreation, pleasure, family property, mutual exchange, personal interaction, healing/cleansing, control and oppression.

▶ Premarital sex among youngsters, though increasing, is still not very significant. Girls tend to be initiated into sex younger due mainly to early marriage. The instances of multiple partners are also not significant. The fact that 47 per cent of women enter into a sexual relationship by the time they have reached 18 years of age (an age at which many remain uneducated and uninformed about sex) makes them vulnerable to unsafe sexual practices, intimidation and violence.

▶ More or less, we can establish the relevance of all available theories and approaches in the analysis and interpretation of Nepali socialization processes with regard to women's bodies, sex and sexuality, as well as attitudes, orientations and behaviour. However, perceptions, attitudes and behaviour are not distributed evenly across social groups and, in fact, it could be said that different Nepali women are living in different time zones. Some, though very few, are talking of sexual rights and decriminalization of sex work, while others are talking about controlling the bodies and sexualities of women. A large group of activists is still focused on socio-economic and political empowerment, which remains the mainstream of activism and advocacy. Those who are talking of sexuality are doing so more from the biomedical perspective, emphasizing reproductive and health issues and the majority of rural women remain very far removed from this activism and discourse.

▶ Sex and sexuality have been, and will continue to be, perennial sources of tension and even violence within and between families. The overall impression is that sexual relations between spouses are largely unbalanced and in the experience of women in particular, less than satisfactory. Instances of marital rape, beating upon refusal of sex, and abuse within families and kin are frequent. Women find it difficult to negotiate a safe and pleasurable sex. Generally, women and girls are not aware of how sex and sexuality are influenced by the patriarchal social order and gender power relations, but they do feel that something is wrong or missing in family and conjugal relations, which makes sexual experience painful rather than pleasurable. Incidence of divorce is increasing. This implies that sexuality education cannot be meaningful unless twinned with gender education.

▸ People are not aware of the linkages between sexuality and empowerment. Even civil society activists have so far failed to articulate this relationship in a concrete and meaningful way so as to exploit its emancipatory potential.

▸ Attitudes towards a woman's sexuality change over time based on her lifecycle. As a virgin girl, as a wife, as a daughter-in-law, as a mother and as a widow, she is expected to negotiate her sexuality in different ways and meet different expectations from her husband, family and society. However, at every stage she is expected to handle her sexuality with great care and in a restrained, 'decent' and 'dignified' way, as prescribed by tradition and the social norms for her age and changing roles. This situation can be attributed to the particular (patriarchal) construction of womanhood and women's sexuality, which, on the whole, is still largely constructed as dangerous, threatening and in need of control and surveillance. Men continue to be haunted by the Freudian syndrome of the split woman embodying the roles of mother and prostitute as objects of both adoration and desire. The ambivalence surrounding the attitudes towards menstruation and fertility, as well as the divine feminine image, if properly exploited, could be used to combat disempowering effects.

▸ Empowering women, especially in countries like Nepal, is clearly crucial in prevention of HIV/AIDS and STDs. It is only by improving women's socio-economic status and addressing the contemporary societal norms, which support unequal sexual exchange, that their vulnerability will be reduced. It will take time to transform women into initiators able to reject a traditional passive femininity and change the entrenched gender power relations so as to ensure that male sexual needs are not catered for at the expense of women's human rights, their safety and pleasure.

- There is a gaping need for sexuality education. Young people feel it particularly important. However, no systematic initiative is in the offing from either the government or the non-government sector; nor are the resources available to fund studies into a relatively new and controversial topic such as women's sexuality in Nepal. The time and space between puberty and wedding night is grey and complex, surrounded by confusion, apprehensions, fantasies, mysteries, taboos, paradoxes and a host of unanswered questions. All bodily possibilities are postponed until one's wedding night. This situation is not conducive to the healthy growth of conjugal relationships. As the family will not be able to handle this issue properly in Nepali society for many years to come, other institutions or agencies, such as schools and NGOs need to step in.

- Of late, the role of audio-visual and print media has been positive and influential in preparing ground for a debate on sexuality, sexual orientation and sexual rights issues. The media has done a great service in legitimizing the cause of sexual minorities and in the gradual building of public opinion. However, the coverage, reach and quality of their engagement are sometimes limited. In any case, if used more imaginatively, the media can be a powerful ally in enlarging campaigns and changing the beliefs, attitudes and behaviour of people towards sex and sexuality.

- Though subsequent democratic governments have become more tolerant towards sexual diversity and they have initiated different policies and legal reforms in recent years, the issues of sexuality, sexual rights, sexual orientation/preference, bodily integrity, personhood and sexuality education remain largely to be addressed. The government does not yet fully recognize the links between sexuality and empowerment. With the growing significance of these issues, we can be optimistic that future policies and legislation will gradually move towards addressing the issues of sexuality in a more comprehensive way.

5 | RECOMMENDATIONS AND THE WAY FORWARD

▸ The first step is to liberate sex and sexuality from its definition as 'dirty, dangerous, destructive and harmful'. This is a necessary step towards developing more positive images of sex and sexuality. This will require a greater debate on the relationship between sexuality and empowerment and the way in which they affect, influence and shape each other's experience.

▸ The second step is to sensitize, inform and educate people and equip them with the basic knowledge, concepts, skills and strategies so as to enable them to identify the liberating and empowering elements of this discourse. This will require the creation and dissemination of liberating knowledge, technologies and practices. It will require greater exploration of the micro-politics of interpersonal relations and the mechanics of patriarchal power at the most intimate level of women's experience, ie in the institutions of marriage, motherhood and heterosexuality, as well as the everyday rituals and regimens that govern women's relationships with themselves, their bodies and men.

▸ The best avenue for sexuality education may be school. Since the government is not yet prepared to embark on such an education programme, civil society should take the lead and develop powerful advocacy networks to effect changes in the government's attitude, policies and programmes. However, as the issue is sensitive, the activists would have to move selectively, cautiously and imaginatively.

▸ Interventions designed to empower should also take into account varying cultural and religious contexts. Most of the people in rural areas are still deeply religious and comply with prescriptions of strictures. They believe in chastity and loyalty, and are haunted by the concept of sin. They believe that their situation is a result of fate, that marriages are made in heaven and that promiscuity or open expressions of sexual inclinations or pleasures are a bad thing. However, they are less aware of the concept, role and manifestations of the divine feminine and the way such concepts and roles can be used to empower them. If education and prevention programmes are to be successful, they have to be informed by culture because different groups of people experience the world differently. Also important is the sexual education of young women and men, to protect their health and reduce the transmission of STDs. Rather than targeting drastic changes within the belief system, as well as in the sexual and behaviour arenas, a gradual approach promoting and teaching condom use and reproductive health, and informed but culturally sensitive debates and education programmes could form the first phase of effective empowerment strategies. This will gradually pave the way for changing the social conditions faced by young girls so as to empower them in the long term to decide on whether or how to have safe sex and so gain control over their body and sexuality.

- A new discourse should be promoted to explore and expose the contradictory stances taken by the Nepali society and culture with regard to women. This debate needs to be taken down to the grass roots level and these contradictions should be deployed as our cultural resource to unmask the hypocrisy, as well as to demystify the invisible patriarchal strategies and mechanisms of control which have been internalized by Nepali society and culture. In doing so, a positive image should be celebrated while deconstructing the current negative image in line with the methods of appreciative inquiry.

- One important aspect is to identify the different needs of different subgroups and subcultures. It would not be a good strategy to launch a 'one size fits all' type of education and empowerment programme. Instead, slight changes will be required to make the education and training tools more relevant and effective in specific localities and subcultures. Particularly, more information needs to be gathered to make the plight of sexual minorities more visible.

- The development of resource books, information and training materials, as well as methodologies that can be used flexibly based on demand, is another critical area of attention. This should be complemented by collaboration with audio-visual and print media. Effective and imaginative mobilization of media can yield surprising outcomes in this arena. They can also be instrumental in making spaces for sexual minorities. The sensitization of political parties, leaders and local social workers is also recommended.

- The stereotypical perception of men as the source of all troubles not only fails to acknowledge the diversity of male experiences of sexuality, but also the operations of disciplinary technologies enacted on them by tradition and culture. What is needed is to provide men with the opportunity to re-examine and reflect upon normative constructs of masculinity, unequal power relations and the core human rights values of dignity and respect. Emerging research points to the usefulness of all-male groups with skilled facilitators creating 'safe places' for men to reflect on social constructs, understand power inequalities and their own misperceptions. Such groups can become effective conduits for changing both perceptions and behaviour. The existence of men's groups such as Pharping men's farmers' cooperative shows great promise for such an approach. Rather than positing men as villains and hostile 'other', building solidarity with them and taking them into confidence as collaborators can be a better and more effective strategy in empowering women sexually. Similarly, rather than launching an education programme as a standalone intervention, it would be more effective if it could be embedded within some kind of livelihood promotion activities.

- The second phase would emphasize promoting new discourses, building constituencies and forging alliances and networks to transform and recreate gender power relations and free the body and sexuality from the shackles of power nexuses and traditionally received knowledge and notions. Foucault's remark that there are no relations of power without resistance is important and instructive. Building resistances at micro level and linking there through a country-wide network can be an effective strategy, which should be launched along with advocacy at the central level. Wider debate is needed to forge solidarity with different kinds of activism so as to harmonize the differing stances concerning sexuality as advanced variously by biomedical, legal–criminal, human rights, *tantric* and social constructionist approaches. Forging networks, sharing lessons and experience, as well as joint strategizing among stakeholders, can create greater impact and synergy.

- Before embracing eroticism, desire and pleasure as legitimate pursuits of human life, it would be advisable to expose the anomalies and contradictions that characterize our culture and behaviour. As indicated above, campaigns for sexuality education, safe sex, HIV/AIDS prevention and sexual and reproductive rights, to name but a few examples, can be entry points to gradually cut out various forms of discrimination and abuse.

- More studies, increased dissemination of findings, wider and more intensive cooperation with the media, other GOs/NGOs and donors, and the use of research findings for advocacy are required. Socially imposed silences regarding the issues of alternative sexualities, as well as the mechanisms of sexual policing and censorship, need to be resisted and challenged.

References

Abbott, Pamela, Claire Wallace and Melissa Tyler. 2005. *Introduction to Sociology: Feminist Perspectives.* London: Routledge Press.

Armas, Henry. 2007. *Whose Sexuality Counts? Poverty, Participation and Sexual Rights.* IDS Working Paper 294. Sussex: Institute of Development Studies.

Baral, Ram Chandra. 2003. 'Pokhara Upatyakama Vivah Vichchhed Nimtyaune Kehi Karak Tatwaharu.' *Contributions to Nepali Studies.* Vol. 30. No. 1. Kathmandu: Centre for Nepal and Asian Studies.

Batliwala, Srilatha. 2006. 'Sexuality and Women's Empowerment: The Fundamental Connection.' In: *Plainspeak.* Issue 2. New Delhi: South and South Asia Resource Centre on Sexuality.

Bennet, Lynn. 1983. *Dangerous Wives and Sacred Sisters: Social and Symbolic Roles of High Caste Women in Nepal.* New York: Columbia University Press.

Bhavnani, Kum-Kum, John Foran and Priya Kurian. 2003. *Feminist Futures: Re-imagining Women, Culture and Development.* Zed Books.

Bista, Dor Bahadur. 2001. *People of Nepal.* Kathmandu: Ratna Pustak Bhandar.

Bryson, Valerie. 2003. *Feminist Political Theory: An Introduction.* Palgrave Macmillan.

Butler, Judith. 1993. *Bodies That Matter: On the Discursive Limits of 'Sex'.* New York: Routledge Press.

Butler, Judith. 1999. *Gender Trouble: Feminism and the Subversion of Identity.* New York and London: Routledge Press.

Capra, Fritjof. 2003. *The Hidden Connections.* The Great Britain: Slamingo.

Carole S. Vance. 1999. 'Anthropology Rediscovers Sexuality: A Theoretical Comment'. In: Richard Parker and Peter Aggleton (eds.) *Culture, Society and Sexuality: A Reader.* Routledge Press.

Dhital, Rupa. 2007. 'Child Marriage in Nepal'. www.cwin.org.np/resources/issues/child_marriage.htm.

Durant, Will. 1935. *The Story of Civilization*. Vol. I. Our Oriental Heritage. New York: Simon and Schuster.

Foucault, M. 1978. *The History of Sexuality: Introduction to Knowledge as Power*. London: Penguin Books Limited.

Foucault, Michel. 1977. *Discipline and Punish: The Birth of the Prison*. London: Allen Lane.

Gautam, RK. 2004. 'STD/HIV/AIDS Prevention in Nepali Schools/ Colleges Youths: Does Peer Education Work?' International Conference on AIDS. Bangkok. http://gateway.nlm.nih.gov/ MeetingAbstracts/ma?f=102277723.html.

Herdt Gilbert, Cymene Howe. 2007. *21st Century Sexualities: Contemporary issues in Health, Education, and Rights*. London: Routledge Press.

Holland, J, Ramazanoglu, C, Scott, S and Thomson, R. 1994. 'Desire, Risk and Control: Body as a site of Contestation.' In: Doyal, L., Naidoo, J., and Wilton, T. (eds) *AIDS: Setting a feminist agenda*. London: Falmer.

Jackson, H. 2002. *AIDS Africa: Continent in Crisis*. Harare: SAfAIDS.

Kakar, Sudhir. 2007. *Indian Identity: Intimate Relations*. New Delhi: Penguin Books.

Kemp, Sandra and Judith Squires. 1998. *Feminisms: Oxford Readers*. New York: Oxford University Press.

Koedt, Anne. 1970. The Myth of the Vaginal Orgasm. http://www. cwluherstory.org/CWLUArchive/vaginalmyth.html

Majpuria, Indra. 1982. *Nepali Women*. Kathmandu: Indra Majpuria.

Majpuria, Indra. 1978. *Marriage Customs in Nepal*. Kathmandu: Indra Majpuria.

Mani, Lata. 2009. *India: Sacred Secular: Contemplative Cultural Critique*. Routeledge India.

McNay, L. 1992. *Foucault and Feminism: Power, Gender and the Self*. Cambridge: Polity Press.

Media Services International (MSI). 2001. A Survey of Teenagers in Nepal: Evaluation Report. http://www.unicef.org/evaldatabase/index_21339. html

Menon, Nivedita (ed). 2007. *Sexualities: Issues in Contemporary Indian Feminism*. New Delhi: Women Unlimited.

Misra, Geetanjali and Radhika Chandiramani (eds). 2007. *Sexuality, Gender and Rights: Eploring Theory and Practice in South and South and Southeast Asia.* New Delhi: Sage Publications.

MoHP, New Era and Macro International, Inc. 2007. *Nepal Demographic Health Survey, 2006.* Kathmandu: Ministry of Health and Population, New Era and Macro International Inc.

Panter-Brick, C. 1986. 'Women's Work and Child Bearing Experience: Two Ethnic Groups of Salme Nepal.' In: *Contributions to Nepali Studies.* Vol. 13. No. 2. Kathmandu: Centre for Nepal and Asian Studies.

Phadke, Shilpa. 2006. 'Space and Sexuality: Thinking Through Some Issues'. In: *Plainspeak.* New Delhi: South and Southeast Asia Resource Centre on Sexuality.

Phelps, Linda. 1979. 'Female Sexual Alienation'. In: Jo Freeman (ed), *Women: A Feminist Perspective.* Second Edition. California: Mayfield Publishing Company.

Pleck, J.H. 1980. 'Men's Power with Women, Other Men and in Society.' In: E.H. Pleck and J.H. Pleck (eds.), *The American Man.* Englewood Cliffs: Prentice Hall.

SAP. 2001. *Commercial Sex Exploitation of Children.* Kathmandu: South Asia Partnership.

Shrestha, Narayan Prasad. 1997. *Kathmandu: The Eternal Kumari.* Kathmandu: Saroz and Kauz.

Tarrier, August. 2005. Bare-Naked Ladies: The Bad Girls of the Post-feminist Nineties.(available at:http://www.electronicbookreview.com/thread/writingpostfeminism/post-feminism).

Thu-Hong, Khuat. 2006. Talking about Sexuality in South and Southeast Asia (Interview). In: *Plainspeak.* Issue 4. New Delhi: South and Southeast Asia Resource Centre on Sexuality.

Vance, Carole S. 1993 (ed). *Pleasure and Danger: Exploring Female Sexuality.* New York: HarperCollins Publishers.